THE AFFORDABLE
KETO
FOR BEGINNERS
#2020

ANNA DAWN

Contents

Why are so many people interested in diets today? Probably because we've become more health-conscious and are looking for ways to maintain health or correct imbalances caused by unhealthy eating habits.

Besides, obesity is spreading like a forest fire and is formally recognized as one of the "diseases of civilization" alongside cancer, stroke, heart diseases, type 2 diabetes, and autoimmune diseases.

But, on top of our generally unhealthy eating habits, there is the ever-present stress which indirectly contributes to unhealthy eating habits.

Keto is one of the "clean eating" trends. A lot has been written about keto and although this is not the easiest of diets, if you want to lose weight quickly, this is the diet for you. The trouble is, you have to be fairly self-disciplined to overcome the crisis you will go through during the first few days.

Although most people struggle for the first week or so, they also very quickly see the first results of this way of eating that serves as a powerful motivation. Unfortunately, healthy foods often cost much more than ordinary foods. This is partly because they are more nutrient-rich, partly because producing healthy foods is sometimes a more labor-intensive process, but also because these foods usually become "in" foods especially if some celebrities claim they've lost a lot of weight using them.

However, it is possible to eat healthy on a budget. You just need to be more self-disciplined when it comes to shopping and better organized when it comes to planning your meals.

Healthy eating should not be the prerogative of the rich. It's possible to eat healthy even on a budget. This book will show you how.

Chapter 1

A ketogenic diet, or Keto, is a low-carb, high-fat, and moderate-protein diet which is based on the theory that if you get most of your calories from fat, rather than carbohydrates, your body will have to burn fat for energy.

The key thing to be aware of with this diet is that if you eat a lot of carbs eg bread, pasta, sweets, etc your body will produce high levels of glucose and insulin. Insulin is needed to carry the glucose throughout the bloodstream. However, as glucose is easily converted into energy, it will be your body's first choice when it needs fuel.

However, once you limit the intake of carbs and proteins, you will force your body to start using alternative sources of energy, ie the fat stored in various parts of your body. That's when your body starts producing ketones and goes into ketosis. This is the main purpose of the ketogenic diet – to reach a state of ketosis.

What is the Ketogenic Diet all About?

To experience most of the benefits of this diet, all you have to do is limit the carbs intake to 50 grams of carbs a day (ideally, it should be only 20 grams). Surviving on so few carbs is not easy, especially in the beginning, but keep in mind that the fewer carbs you take, the sooner will you reach ketosis and start losing weight.

However, don't force this diet upon yourself at all costs, for it does not suit everyone. Be particularly careful if you are on chronic medication or suffer from a chronic condition that could be made worse with a drastic reduction of carbs. In either case, it's best to consult your medical practitioner before deciding to try keto. Besides, to stay healthy with so few carbs and protein, you have to work out how to compensate the nutrients you're deprived of.

The foods you are not supposed to eat on this diet include, unfortunately, most of the foods we eat a lot of, e.g. grains, sweets, fruits, starches, beans, legumes, etc. The trick to succeeding with a keto diet is to avoid or limit these foods but stay healthy.

When you first go on a keto diet, your body will be in a shock for the first few days and you may constantly have headaches, feel irritable or be generally weak. Fortunately, these symptoms of keto-adaptation will go away after a week or so.

The easiest way of reaching ketosis, and starting to burn fat, is to follow the basic principles of the ketogenic lifestyle.

8 steps to reaching ketosis:

1)   **Restrict carbohydrates in your diet**
You shouldn't take more than 50 gr of carbs per day, although taking only 20 gr would be idea.

2)   Limit protein intake
If weight-loss is the main reason you follow the ketogenic diet, you shouldn't take more than about 100 gr protein per day.

3)   Increase fat intake
If you reduce carbs, you have to increase the intake of fats so your body always has the fuel to run on. Besides, food rich in fats will make you feel full, which will help you avoid sugar cravings.

4)   **Drink water**
Drink as much water as you can. It's best to drink warm water because it provides better hydration than the cold one.

5)   Stop snacking
Cut down even on healthy snacks, if you're trying to lose weight.

6)   Try intermittent fasting
Fasting will boost your ketone levels, and enable you to reach ketosis, which will force your body to burn fat.

7)   Exercise
To lose weight quickly, you have to combine dieting with physical activity.

8)   Take supplements
Supplements will help with some of the side-effects during the keto-adaptation period.

When can you expect to reach ketosis?

This depends mainly on whether you manage to stick to this diet without cheating. The easiest way to check if you've reached ketosis is to have your urine or blood checked with urine or blood strips. However, the urine strips are not very accurate, so rather watch out for the telltale symptoms of ketosis:

5 symptoms of ketosis:

–   Increased urination
–   Dry mouth
–   Bad breath
–   Loss of appetite
–   Increased energy

The main reason the ketogenic diet is so popular is that it makes it possible to lose a lot of weight quickly – in a healthy way. This is the main reason why there's been such an interest in this diet.

Another reason for the popularity of keto lifestyle is that many health conditions can benefit from this diet, eg cancer, heart disease, diabetes, epilepsy, Alzheimer's, Parkinson's, some autoimmune disorders, etc.

However, even if you don't suffer from any life-threatening diseases, you can benefit from the keto diet simply because it will help you improve both your mental and physical performance, stay in shape and get rid of cravings.

So, the keto diet is not only about weight management. It is as much about disease prevention and reversal of many chronic diseases that plague modern society.

Anna Dawn

Chapter 2

Keto Diet on a Budget

Most healthy diets are about healthy foods and healthy eating habits. However, there is one problem. Healthy foods are usually more expensive than regular foods. Does this mean healthy eating should be the prerogative of the rich?

Healthy foods are more expensive for a reason. They are usually higher in nutrients and can help you feel full for longer. Or, the core ingredients are more expensive, eg almond flour vs grain flour. Besides, they are often produced in more labor-intensive ways. Then, some of the healthy foods, are imported from far-away countries, eg tapioca flour, etc

When you study keto recipes, you'll see that many of them are based on pricey ingredients. So, is it possible to eat keto on a budget?

Of course it is, but it takes some forward planning and careful budgeting.

<u>8 tips for creating a keto diet on a budget</u>

1.   Buy in bulk
If you decide to start saving on groceries, the first thing to do is start buying in bulk, especially at places like Costco, Walmart, Sam's Club, etc.

Stock up on non-perishables, such as coconut milk, seasonings, healthy oils, dried or frozen foods, etc. In the case of perishables, such as meat and fish, you can buy in stock if you come across a good deal, and keep it in the deep-freeze.

2.   Cook in bulk
Batch cooking means you always have something to eat if you don't feel like cooking. Besides, cooling in bulk saves both time and money. You cook from ingredients that are on sale or are in season at the moment, and you prepare several dishes that you can eat throughout the week.

3.   Look for discounts
Many stores offer special deals on foods near the expiration date. You can save a lot this way so get into the habit of paying attention to flyers and in-

store promotional materials.

4.   Stick to your shopping list

To make sure you don't buy on impulse and also to ensure you buy everything you need for your keto meals, never go shopping without a shopping list. And stick to it!

5.   Shop online

Shopping online can save a lot of money, especially on the so-called healthy foods such as nuts, almond four, coconut flour, chia seeds, etc. *Amazon* is a good place to start but you can also check *Thrive Market*, *Whole Foods, Nuts.com,* and *ButcherBox.*

6.   Create your keto menu with affordable foods in mind

If your budget is very tight, find out what the price of foods you should be eating most of are, eg broccoli, cauliflower, cabbage, spinach, avocado, etc. Then look for recipes that are based on these foods.

Whenever possible, buy frozen instead of fresh produce because you can save a lot that way. When it comes to meat, choose affordable cuts of meat or buy in bulk and freeze for later use.

7.   Analyze your grocery bill

Get into the habit of checking your grocery bill on a weekly or monthly basis to make sure it does not include items that shouldn't be there, eg latte, energy drinks, expensive wine, unhealthy snacks, etc. If you're living on a budget, quit drinking, and stick to water.

8.   Cook from scratch

First of all, start buying whole vs chopped/peeled/washed foods. Start making your own salad dressings, sauces, nut butters, soups, etc from scratch. You will save money and avoid the food additives that these foods are full of.

Buy the whole chicken (or other meat) instead of boneless, skinless chicken breasts. Buy the whole stalk of celery, broccoli or carrots instead of pre-chopped veggies. Buy whole almonds instead of peeled and sliced ones. Avoiding "convenient" foods could save you a fortune over a twelve-month period.

Chapter 3

Planning Your Weekly Shopping

Eating keto will affect your lifestyle because to live the keto way, you have to become more organized. You also need to be educated enough to know how to calculate your macros. And if on top of that you want to eat keto on a budget, you'll have to do even better than that.

Keto on a budget revolves around three issues:

1.   Planning

This phase involves collecting keto recipes you would like to try or creating your own. Please note, that when living on a budget, you should stay away from fancy meals or meals with lots of ingredients. The next step is to create a weekly menu and work out what ingredients you'll need for those meals.

2.   Shopping

Get into the habit of never going shopping without a shopping list, especially if you're trying to live on a budget. Take into account all the meals you will need to prepare in the following week plus snacks or foods for unexpected visitors. Shop at discount stores if you are shopping in bulk. Be on the look-out for sales even if that means changing your meal plans for that week. It pays to be flexible when creating a menu and when it comes to fresh fruits and vegetables, eat only what's in season.

3.   Meal preparation the keto way

Although convenience foods are usually very tasty and convenient, such meals are usually much more expensive than home-made ones. However, as cooking from scratch takes a lot of time, try to make your life easier by getting appliances like food processors, crock pots, a vacuum sealing machine, storage containers, etc that will make cooking easier. If you are short of time, cooking in batch will help a lot both in terms of time and money.

Avoid or limit meals that require special ingredients, eg coconut, almond or tapioca flour, artificial sweeteners, imported vegetables, etc because these are not cheap. Try to stay away from ingredients available only in health food shops as these are usually more expensive than the same ingredients available from regular shops. If your menu consists of meat recipes, be prepared to go for cheaper cuts of meat, eg the fattier cuts. This is not as bad as it seems because on keto you need to increase the amount of fat in your diet.

To further save on food, buy only the food you know you will eat. We often buy foods we think we should eat because it is healthy, although deep-down we hate such foods.

If you want to cook from scratch, or cook in bulk, remember that you'll have to set aside one day a week to cook for the rest of the week. Although spending Sundays in a kitchen may not be your idea of fun, if you're very busy and usually get home late, if you cook in bulk, you'll always have a healthy meal waiting for you even when you come home too exhausted to cook.

It's best to focus on simple meals that do not require a lot of ingredients. One of the ways of saving money without eating the same meals over and over again is to change seasonings instead of ingredients. With the change of spices, you can turn a simple dish into a Chinese stir fry, Indian curry, Hungarian paprikash, Thai-style fish, Italian-style shrimp, etc.

Chapter 4

Under $20 Per Week Shopping Ideas

Often, it's not what you buy but where and when you buy it. Certain foods tend to be more expensive at certain times of the year (eg when they are out of season, or before certain holidays) or in certain shops (eg health food shops are generally more expensive than regular shops).

When you live on a budget, it becomes even more important where you shop for ingredients. However, if you enjoy cooking and shopping for food, it will take a lot of self-discipline to shop for under $20 for a week.

9 key rules to stick to:

1.   **Take only the money you had budgeted for the week, eg $20**
It's well-known that people generally spend much more money than they had originally planned if they pay with credit cards. Or, if they take more money with them, just in case. This is why, if trying to live on a budget, you should use only cash and not take more money with you than what you intend to spend.

2.   **Don't go shopping without a shopping list**
When you shop on impulse, you are bound to forget some of the ingredients you were supposed to buy but you are also much more likely to buy what you shouldn't, eg unhealthy snacks, comfort foods, soda, etc.

3.   **If the list is unrealistic, prioritize**
If the shopping list contains more articles that you think you can squeeze into $20, prioritize the items on the list so you buy only what's essential for healthy meals for a week.

4.   **If something is on sale, buy it even if you hadn't planned to cook it that week**
The trick with saving on grocery shopping is using an opportunity when it presents itself. So, if you stumble upon a sale of an item you hadn't planned for that week, eg fish, buy it and change your menu. Try food chains like Walmart, Kroger, and Amazon for best deals.

5.   **Stop eating out**
This could save you a lot of money. So, instead of meeting friends for lunch or dinner someplace, invite them to your place and prepare a meal

together. It's fun, it will improve your bond with your friends, and it's much, much cheaper.

6. *Stock up*
If space allows, stock up on canned, dried or frozen foods, potatoes, apples, oranges, and everything else that is cheaper to in bulk and that can last for a while.

7. **When it comes to fresh fruits and veggies, buy only what's in season**
Not only are seasonal fruits and vegetables cheaper, they are also fresher and tastier.

8. *Use coupons*
Look for coupons in newspapers, magazines, and in stores and regularly check for promotions.
"

9. *Use soup kitchens*
These are not just for the homeless, anyone can eat there although most people wouldn't like to be seen using one. However, if you are struggling to survive on just $20 per week, this is one of the options.

10. *Cook from scratch*
Home-made bread, soup, roast or pasta dish are much cheaper from those available in shops. And if you know how to cook, they can be tastier too. Enroll on a cooking course or ask a friend to teach you.

Chapter 5

Eating healthy, home-cooked meals is not something everyone can look forward to. Not just because they can't cook but because cooking and baking from scratch usually takes a lot of time. The solution is to learn about meal prepping.

Meal prepping is the art of forward planning. By creating a few meals (when you have time) and spreading them out throughout the week (to use them when you don't have time to cook) you are saving yourself a lot of time and money. You can do this by stocking up on staples that you will need for various meals throughout the week, eg frozen veggies, meat, cheese, eggs, etc) or by setting aside one day a week to cook for the whole week.

Meal prepping in 4 steps:

1.   Start by working out how many meals you will need for that week, ie how many breakfasts, lunches, dinners, and snacks and for how many people. If you more or less have an idea of what you will be eating for those meals, you can save a lot to time if you stock up on what you will be using the most of. If possible, you can pre-prepare some foods before freezing them so the actual cooking time is significantly reduced.

2.   If you are new to cooking or are very busy, avoid trying to cook meals that require many ingredients. Focus on veggies, one protein and lots of healthy fats.

3.   If you are new to meal prepping or cooking, this may be too much for you ie planning for 7 lunches, 7 dinners, 7 breakfasts, etc especially if you're prepping for more than just yourself. In that case, focus only on one meal per day. For example, until you get into the spirit of meal prepping, focus on stocking up for 7 dinners, or lunches, or breakfasts.

4.   Use only simple recipes and simple cooking methods, eg soups, stews, stir-fries, etc.

However, if you work from home, are retired or are a stay-at-home mom, you probably do have more time so you can be more relaxed about both shopping and meal preparation. You can make each of your meals fresh, cooking what you feel like eating on that particular day. Meal prepping is primarily for the very busy and the well-organized.

However, there's not much point in shopping for healthy and affordable ingredients and preparing healthy meals if they are not stored properly. So, here are some of the containers you can use:

– Airtight containers (silicone or stainless steel)

– Microwavable containers (make sure they are BPA-free)

– Freezer-safe containers (they prevent nutrient loss)

– Leak-proof, compartmentalized containers (good for meals where ingredients are added at the last minute.

Besides, depending on what kind of meals you plan to take for lunch, you may decide to invest in a cooler or insulated meal bag. This becomes even more important if, due to your lifestyle, you are often away from home from early morning until late at night. In that case, what you need is not just lunch, but two or three meals. One of the benefits of meal prepping is that when you pack your lunch you can make your meals as varied and as healthy as you want to, even if you are often on the road or work long and unsociable hours.

Chapter 6

Shopping Tips to Save Money

When it comes to saving money on grocery shopping, the secret lies in planning ahead. If you do, you will save time, money, and buy the foods you actually need. There are many different suggestions on how to go about grocery shopping on a budget. While this will largely depend on your circumstances, it all boils down to two things.

2 things to focus on when grocery shopping on a budget:

1.   What you are shopping for (eg all three meals for the whole week, just dinner for a week, just breakfast and dinner, etc)

2.   How you are going to use the food you buy (eg are you going to cook the food you buy; or are you only buying ingredients you can use in salads, muesli or smoothies, eg fruits, vegetables, and nuts & seeds; or are you buying in bulk to freeze or preserve in some way).

So, don't shop on impulse, shop with a plan. That's the only way you will manage to get the foods you need for a keto diet at the prices you can afford.

How to Organise Your Grocery Shopping:

1.   Plan your meals for the week and make a shopping list accordingly.

2.   When planning meals, make sure you have some leftovers you can use for lunch the following day.

3.   Shopping can be exhausting, so don't do it if you've had a very busy and difficult day or if you're feeling unwell.

4.   Stick to your shopping list (which is not easy if your children are with you).

5.   You will save a lot of money if you pack your own lunch. If you buy lunch, it will cost you at least $100 a month. Over 12 months, it's a small fortune. Besides, when you bring a packed lunch you can use any leftovers

you have at home, you can prepare a healthy meal, and you also save time because you don't waste time getting lunch.

6.   Gradually, try to wean yourself off buying canned and packaged convenience foods, eg shredded cabbage or cheese, peeled potatoes, chopped carrots, etc.

7.   If you find a good deal and decide to buy large quantities of meat, make sure you know how to store it so it lasts. One of the ways to speed up meal preparation time after defrosting meat is to pre-cook or marinate the meat before freezing.
8.   Don't do grocery shopping on the run. Make a plan when you're going to shop for the week.

9.   Be prepared to try new foods if you find good deals.

10.   Learn how to cook and bake from scratch.

11.   Don't feel embarrassed to shop at discount stores whenever you can.

12.   Buy only what you need and what you're going to use. Sometimes a good grocery deal may offer you 3 of something, or 100 eggs, etc. Before you accept any such deals, make sure you know how to use or store the stuff you buy.

13.   No-name goods are often as good as the branded ones.

14.   What's on sale is not always a good deal. Shop around especially if you're buying in bulk.

Chapter 7

Meal Prep Tips to Prevent Wastage

As the world gets richer, food wastage becomes a major problem. Of course, there is a huge difference in how much food is wasted in developed countries, particularly in the US, and how much in the rest of the world. But even so, far too much food is being thrown away.

According to statistics, about 1/3 of all the food produced in the world is wasted. That is over a billion tons of food – per year. This means that hundreds of millions of dollars are thrown away every year while at the same time, millions are undernourished – even in the developed world.

However, wasting food is much more than wasting money. Discarded food is taken to landfills, where it rots and produces methane gas. This means that the food we throw out indirectly contributes to climate change.

Besides, food production requires a lot of water. About 70% of all water taken from rivers and groundwater sources is used for irrigation and on meat farms. Of that amount, about 25% is wasted through food-waste every year.

All this shows that wasting food should be considered a serious crime. When you throw food away, you pollute the environment and contribute to the depletion of our water resources.

The worst thing is that it doesn't have to be like this. There are many ways to reduce your food waste, either by using less or by reusing and recycling.

Depending on your circumstances you may or may not be able to follow these tips on how to reduce food waste. However, just remember that when you don't waste food you are not only helping the environment, you are also saving a lot of money.

17 tips on how to reduce food wastage:

1. Don't buy more than you need

2. Don't go shopping when you're hungry, angry, or upset because that's

when you are most likely to buy more food than you need, a lot of which will be comfort food

3. It's more difficult to buy exactly how much you need if you're buying in bulk. So, if you shop this way toy save mone, at least make sure you first use all of the food you've already bought. If you can't use it, find a way to preserve it.

4. It's easier to plan food shopping for a couple of days than for a week so if you can, shop twice a week rather than just once. If you shop once a month (as many people do), you usually either don't get enough food or you get far too much. If possible, try to avoid shopping on a monthly basis.

5. Get into the habit of using up all the food you already have before getting new supplies.

6. Don't go shopping without a shopping list.

7. Learn old fashioned ways of preserving food, eg learn how to make jam, juice, chutney, sauerkraut, pickled vegetables, cured meat, etc.

8. Keeping your fridge overstocked is how food often goes to waste. Go through it at least once a month.

9. Don't throw away leftovers. You can use them for lunch the following day or you can freeze them for later use.

10. Eat all of it, ie eat the whole egg or fruit. Many people discard the egg yolk in order to lower their cholesterol levels, however, unless you have extremely high cholesterol, it's safe to eat the whole egg because it is the yolk where all the nutrients are. Don't peel the fruits such as apple, pear, peach, etc because the skin is where most of the vitamins and antioxidants are.

11. Store food correctly so it lasts longer. Statistics show that about 2/3 of all the food produced is wasted due to inadequate storage. Learn how to avoid premature ripening, or what foods should never be kept in a fridge, eg potatoes, tomatoes, garlic, cucumbers, and onions.

12. Certain foods produce a lot of ethylene gas. This promotes ripening in foods and often leads to spoilage. These foods are bananas, avocados, tomatoes, peaches, etc. Keep these foods away from ethylene-sensitive foods such as potatoes, apples, leafy greens, berries and peppers to avoid premature spoilage. Or, you can use foods that produce more ethylene gas to make other foods ripen faster by keeping them in a paper bag together

for a couple of days.

13. Veggies leftovers are full of fiber and other nutrients so instead of throwing them away, you can use them in smoothies, eg chopped broccoli stalks, vegetable peels, wilted herbs, overripe bananas, etc. You can also use fruit and vegetable peels to make water taste better, eg apple skins, cucumber slices, citrus fruits, etc. Needless to say, these fruits and vegetables should be first washed carefully.

14. If you don't have a freezer, or if the food leftovers cannot be frozen, you can compost them. That way, food waste becomes food for plants.

15, You can use coffee grounds as a plant fertilizer or a natural mosquito repellent. Sprinkling spent coffee grounds onto the grass where mosquito are likely to be, will deter female mosquitos from laying eggs there.

16. Be creative when it comes to food leftovers. Learn how to use parts of vegetables you normally throw away, eg stems, stalks, soft tomatoes, wilted greens, etc to prepare new meals. You can use them to make soup, pesto, or add them to stews.

17. To save money on beauty products and avoid food waste, you can use food leftovers to create original and 100% natural beauty products

For example, you can use overripe bananas, avocados, peach, tomato, strawberries, apple, and almost all other fruits to prepare a refreshing face mask.

If you add an egg yolk, a little bit of milk, sour cream, or honey to the mashed fruit, you get a very nutritious face mask. You can also use coffee leftovers as a body scrub.

Or, you can apply used tea bags or leftover cucumber slices to your eyes to reduce puffiness.

Anna Dawn

Sample Week (Week 6)

Shopping List for Week 6

Look in pantry for:

- Minced garlic
- Himalayan pink salt/sea salt
- Organic garlic powder
- Organic ginger powder
- Organic onion powder
- Organic black pepper
- Organic red pepper flakes
- Organic cayenne pepper
- Organic paprika
- Organic dried oregano
- Organic dried basil
- Organic rosemary
- Stevia
- Sriracha sauce
- Fish sauce
- Sesame seeds
- Soy sauce, low-sodium
- Apple cider vinegar
- Olive oil
- Sesame oil

Purchase the following:

Items:	Store	Quantity	Price ($)
Large White Eggs, 12 count	Walmart	1	1.19
Turkey Bacon, 12 Oz.	Walmart	1	2.21
Shredded Cheddar Cheese, 8 oz	Walmart	1	1.54
Cauliflower head 1 pound	Walmart	1	1.98
Chicken Sausage in Chicken Broth 8.2 Ounce	Walmart	1	0.58
Brussels Sprouts, 12 oz	Walmart	1	1.07
Boneless Skinless Chicken thighs, 2.5 lb. 8 count	Walmart	1	5.21

Tomato Sauce with Basil Garlic and Oregano 8 oz	Walmart	1	0.5
Whipped Topping 8 oz	Walmart	1	0.73
Ground turkey 1 lb.	Walmart	1	1.51
Tri-Color Cole Slaw, 16 oz	Walmart	1	1.03
Avocado 6 count	Walmart	1	2.04
Lemon	Walmart	1	0.38
		Total:	19.97

Day 1

Breakfast – Avocado Egg Boat with Cheddar

Serving: 2
Preparation time: 5 minutes; Cooking time: 15 minutes
Nutritional Info: 263.5 Cal; 21.4 g Fats; 12 g Protein; 1.3 g Net Carb; 4.6 g Fiber;
Ingredients
- 1 avocado, halved, pitted
- 2 eggs
- 2 tablespoons chopped bacon
- 2 tablespoons shredded cheddar cheese

Extra:
- 1/8 teaspoon salt
- 1/8 teaspoon ground black pepper

Directions
- Switch on the oven, then set it to 400 degrees F and let it preheat.
- Meanwhile, prepare avocado and for this, cut it into half lengthwise and then remove the pit.
- Scoop out some of the flesh from the center, crack an egg into each half, then sprinkle with bacon and season with salt and black pepper.
- Sprinkle cheese over egg and avocado and then bake for 10 to 15 minutes or until the yolk has cooked to desired level.
- Serve straight away.

Lunch – Roasted Cauliflower Steaks

Serving: 2
Preparation time: 5 minutes; Cooking time: 20 minutes
Nutritional Info: 176 Cal; 13.8 g Fats; 4.3 g Protein; 6.7 g Net Carb; 5.4 g Fiber;
Ingredients
- ¼ of a cauliflower head
- ½ teaspoon minced garlic
- 2 tablespoons olive oil
- 2 tablespoons grated cheddar cheese

Extra:
- 1/8 teaspoon red pepper flakes
- ¼ teaspoon salt
- 1/8 teaspoon ground black pepper

Directions
- Switch on the oven, then set it to 400 degrees F and let it preheat.
- Meanwhile, prepare cauliflower steaks and for this, cut it into two slices and place them onto a baking sheet lined with parchment paper.
- Place oil in a small bowl, add remaining ingredients except for cheese, stir well and then brush half of the mixture on top of the cauliflower.
- Bake cauliflower for 10 minutes, then flip them, brush with remaining olive oil mixture, sprinkle with cheese and then continue baking for 10 minutes until roasted.
- Serve straight away.

Dinner – Brussels sprouts with Sausage

Serving: 2
Preparation time: 5 minutes; Cooking time: 18 minutes
Nutritional Info: 130.5 Cal; 10 g Fats; 6 g Protein; 2.3 g Net Carb; 1.6 g Fiber;

Ingredients
- 2 ounces sausage, diced
- 3 ounces Brussel sprouts, halved
- 1 tablespoon olive oil
- ¼ cup of water

Extra:
- 1/3 teaspoon salt
- 1/4 teaspoon ground black pepper

Directions
- Take a skillet pan, place it over medium heat, add oil and when hot, add diced sausage and cook for 3 minutes until golden brown.
- Add sprouts, pour in water, season with salt and black pepper, and cook for 7 to 10 minutes until sprouts are just tender, covering the pan.
- Then uncover the pan, switch heat to medium-high level and continue cooking for 2 to 3 minutes or until all the liquid in the pan has evaporated and Brussel sprouts are golden brown.
- Serve straight away.

Day 2
Breakfast – Cauliflower Fritters

Serving: 2
Preparation time: 5 minutes; Cooking time: 8 minutes
Nutritional Info: 92 Cal; 7.2 g Fats; 4.6 g Protein; 2 g Net Carb; 1.3 g Fiber;
Ingredients
- ½ cup cauliflower florets
- 3 tablespoons shredded cheddar cheese
- ½ of egg
- 1 tablespoon olive oil

Extra:
- ¼ teaspoon salt
- 1/8 teaspoon ground black pepper

Directions
- Take a food processor, add cauliflower florets in it, then pulse them until finely chopped and tip the florets into a heatproof bowl.
- Cover the bowl with a plastic wrap, pork holes by using a fork and then microwave for 2 minutes or until just tender.

- Then add remaining ingredients except for oil and stir well until incorporated and cheese has melted.
- Take a skillet pan, place it over medium heat, add oil and when hot, drop in ¼ of the batter, shape it into patties and cook for 3 minutes per side until crispy and browned.
- Serve straight away.

Lunch – Cheesy Bacon Wrapped Chicken

Serving: 2
Preparation time: 5 minutes; Cooking time: 25 minutes
Nutritional Info: 172.5 Cal; 11.5 g Fats; 14.5 g Protein; 0.5 g Net Carb; 0 g Fiber;
Ingredients
- 2 chicken thighs, boneless
- 2 strips of bacon
- 2 tablespoons shredded cheddar cheese

Extra:
- 1/3 teaspoon salt
- 2/3 teaspoon paprika
- 1/4 teaspoon garlic powder

Directions
- Switch on the oven, then set it to 400 degrees F and let it preheat.
- Meanwhile, season chicken thighs with salt, paprika, and garlic on both sides, and then place them onto a baking sheet greased with oil.
- Top each chicken thighs with a bacon strip and then bake for 15 to 20 minutes until the chicken has cooked through, and bacon has crispy.
- When done, sprinkle cheese over chicken, continue baking for 5 minutes until cheese has melted and golden, and then serve.

Dinner – Baked Sausage

Serving: 2
Preparation time: 5 minutes; Cooking time: 20 minutes
Nutritional Info: 137.5 Cal; 12.3 g Fats; 5.3 g Protein; 0.8 g Net Carb; 0.5 g Fiber;
Ingredients
- 3-ounce chicken sausage
- 2 tablespoons tomato sauce
- 3 tablespoons cheddar cheese
- 3 ounces whipped topping

Extra:
- ¼ teaspoon salt
- 1/8 teaspoon ground black pepper

Directions
- Switch on the oven, then set it to 400 degrees F and let it preheat.
- Take a baking dish, grease it with oil, place chicken sausages in it, and then bake for 15 minutes.
- Meanwhile, prepare the sauce and for this, place tomato sauce in a bowl, add whipped topping and stir until well mixed.
- When chicken sausages have cooked, spread prepared sauce over them, sprinkle with cheese, and cook for 5 minutes until cheese has melted and golden brown.
- Serve straight away.

Day 3

Breakfast – Brussel Sprouts Bacon Breakfast Hash

Serving: 2

Preparation time: 5 minutes; Cooking time: 25 minutes
Nutritional Info: 134.5 Cal; 8.2 g Fats; 10.8 g Protein; 2.8 g Net Carb; 1.6 g Fiber;
Ingredients

1. 3 ounces Brussel sprouts, sliced
2. 2 slices of bacon, chopped
3. ½ teaspoon minced garlic
4. ¾ tablespoon apple cider vinegar
5. 2 eggs

Directions

- Place a skillet pan over medium heat and when hot, add bacon and cook for 5 to 7 minutes until crispy.
- Transfer bacon to a plate, add garlic and cook for 30 seconds until fragrant.
- Then add Brussel sprouts, stir in vinegar and cook for 5 minutes until tender.
- Return bacon into the pan, cook for 5 minutes until sprouts are golden brown, then create a well in the pan and cracks the egg in it.
- Cook the eggs for 3 to 5 minutes until cooked to the desired level and then serve immediately.

Lunch – Egg Roll Bowl

Serving: 2
Preparation time: 5 minutes; Cooking time: 8 minutes
Nutritional Info: 144.8 Cal; 9.7 g Fats; 11.2 g Protein; 2 g Net Carb; 1 g Fiber;
Ingredients

1. ¼ pound ground turkey
2. ½ teaspoon minced garlic
3. 6-ounce coleslaw mix
4. 2/3 tablespoon apple cider vinegar
5. 1 teaspoon olive oil

Extra:

6. ½ teaspoon salt
7. ½ tablespoon soy sauce
8. 1 tablespoon water
9. 1 teaspoon sesame oil

Directions

- Take a skillet pan, place it over medium heat, add olive oil and when hot, add ground turkey and cook for 5 minutes until browned.

- Add garlic, stir, and cook for 30 seconds until fragrant, add coleslaw mix and water, toss until well mixed and cook for 2 minutes until coleslaw has softened.
- Place soy sauce and vinegar in a small bowl, add sesame oil and salt and then stir until well mixed.
- Drizzle the soy sauce mixture on coleslaw mixture, toss until combined and remove the pan from heat.
- Serve straight away.

Dinner – Sesame Chicken Thighs

Serving: 2
Preparation time: 5 minutes; Cooking time: 20 minutes
Nutritional Info: 130 Cal; 8.8 g Fats; 10.7 g Protein; 0.7 g Net Carb; 1.3 g Fiber;
Ingredients

- 2 chicken thighs, boneless
- 2 teaspoons soy sauce
- 4 tablespoons sesame seeds

Extra:

- ½ teaspoon garlic powder
- 1 tablespoon apple cider vinegar
- ½ teaspoon ginger powder

Directions

- Switch on the oven, then set it to 375 degrees F and let it preheat.
- Meanwhile, prepare the sauce and for this, place soy sauce and vinegar in a small bowl, add garlic powder and ginger powder and stir until combined.
- Place chicken thighs in a plastic bag, pour in the sauce, seal the bag and turn the bag upside down until chicken has coated with the sauce.
- Place sesame seeds in a shallow dish, dredge chicken thighs in it until covered, then place chicken into a baking dish greased with oil and bake for 15 to 20 minutes until thoroughly cooked.
- Serve straight away.

Day 4
Breakfast – Sausage and Fried Eggs

Serving: 2
Preparation time: 5 minutes; Cooking time: 18 minutes
Nutritional Info: 100 Cal; 100 g Fats; 100 g Protein; 100 g Net Carb; 100 g Fiber;
Ingredients
- 2 sausage links
- 2 eggs
- 1 teaspoon olive oil

Extra:
- ¼ teaspoon salt
- ¼ teaspoon ground black pepper

Directions
- Take a skillet pan, place it over medium heat, add oil and when hot, add sausage and cook for 5 to 8 minutes until golden brown on all sides.
- Push sausage to a side, then crack eggs in it and cook for 3 to 5 minutes per side until cooked to the desired level.
- Transfer sausage and eggs to two serving plates, season with salt and black pepper, and then serve.

Lunch – Sweet and Spicy Brussel Sprouts

Serving: 2
Preparation time: 5 minutes; Cooking time: 12 minutes
Nutritional Info: 98.5 Cal; 7.8 g Fats; 1.7 g Protein; 3.4 g Net Carb; 2 g Fiber;
Ingredients
- 3 ounces Brussel Sprouts, halved
- ¾ tablespoon soy sauce

- ¾ tablespoons liquid stevia
- ½ tablespoon Sriracha sauce
- ¾ teaspoon sesame seeds

Extra:
- 1 tablespoon olive oil
- ¼ teaspoon salt

Directions
- Prepare the sauce, and for this, place soy sauce in a bowl, add maple syrup, Sriracha sauce, and stir until mixed.
- Take a skillet pan, place it over medium heat, add oil and when hot, add Brussel sprouts and cook for 7 to 10 minutes until nicely golden brown.
- Then pour in prepared sauce in the last 2 minutes of cooking, toss until well coated, and continue cooking until done.
- Season Brussel sprouts with salt, sprinkle with sesame seeds and then serve,

Dinner – Taco Minced

Serving: 2
Preparation time: 5 minutes; Cooking time: 12 minutes
Nutritional Info: 164 Cal; 8 g Fats; 11 g Protein; 4 g Net Carb; 3 g Fiber;
Ingredients
- 4 ounces ground turkey
- 1/8 teaspoon garlic powder
- 1/8 teaspoon onion powder
- 2 tablespoons water
- 3 ounces tomato sauce

Extra:
- 1 tablespoon olive oil
- ¼ teaspoon salt
- ¾ teaspoon red chili powder
- 1/3 teaspoon cumin

Directions
- Take a skillet pan, place it over medium heat and when hot, add turkey and cook for 5 to 8 minutes until nicely browned.
- Drain the grease, add remaining ingredients and simmer for 2 to 3 minutes until thick and done.
- Serve straight away.

Day 5
Breakfast – Bacon Sandwich

Serving: 2
Preparation time: 5 minutes; Cooking time: 20 minutes
Nutritional Info: 251.3 Cal; 22.1 g Fats; 12 g Protein; 0.4 g Net Carb; 1 g Fiber;
Ingredients

- 4 slices of bacon
- 2 eggs, fried
- ½ of a medium avocado, sliced
- 2 tablespoons tomato sauce

Directions

- Switch on the oven, then set it to 375 degrees F and let it preheat.
- Meanwhile, cut each bacon slice into six strips, then weave three horizontal bacon strips with three vertical bacon strips to create one slice of the sandwich; create three more sandwich slices in the same manner.
- Place the bacon slices onto a baking sheet lined with parchment paper and bake for 15 to 20 minutes until bacon has thoroughly cooked.
- When done, pat dry bacon slices with a paper towel, let them rest for 5 minutes until crispy, and then prepare the sandwich.
- For this, top two slices of bacon with a fried egg, then layer with avocado slices and add 1 tablespoon tomato sauce.
- Cover the top with remaining bacon slices and serve.

Lunch – Beans and Sausage

Serving: 2
Preparation time: 5 minutes; Cooking time: 6 minutes
Nutritional Info: 151 Cal; 9.4 g Fats; 11.7 g Protein; 3.4 g Net Carb; 1.6 g Fiber;
Ingredients

- 4 ounces green beans
- 4 ounces chicken sausage, sliced
- ½ teaspoon dried basil
- ½ teaspoon dried oregano
- 1/3 cup chicken broth, from chicken sausage

Extra:
- 1 tablespoon olive oil
- ¼ teaspoon salt
- 1/8 teaspoon ground black pepper

Directions
- Switch on the instant pot, place all the ingredients in its inner pot and shut with lid, in the sealed position.
- Press the "manual" button, cook for 6 minutes at high-pressure settings and, when done, do quick pressure release.
- Serve immediately.

Dinner – Lemon-Rosemary Chicken

Serving: 2
Preparation time: 5 minutes; Cooking time: 6 minutes
Nutritional Info: 97.5 Cal; 6.6 g Fats; 8.8 g Protein; 0.1 g Net Carb; 0.7 g Fiber;
Ingredients
- 2 chicken thighs, boneless
- ½ of a lemon, juiced, zested
- 1 teaspoon chopped rosemary
- ½ teaspoon minced garlic
- 1 tablespoon olive oil

Extra:
- 1/3 teaspoon salt
- 1/4 teaspoon ground black pepper

Directions
- Take a grill pan, place it over medium-high heat, grease it with oil and let it preheat.
- Meanwhile, place chicken thighs in a plastic bag, add remaining ingredients in it, seal the bag and turn it upside down until evenly coated.
- Transfer chicken onto the grill pan, cook for 3 minutes per side until thoroughly cooked and then serve.

Day 6
Breakfast – Eggs in Clouds

Serving: 2
Preparation time: 5 minutes; Cooking time: 5 minutes
Nutritional Info: 101 Cal; 7.1 g Fats; 8.6 g Protein; 0.8 g Net Carb; 0 g Fiber;
Ingredients
- 2 eggs
- 2 tablespoons chopped bacon, cooked

Extra:
- ¼ teaspoon salt
- 1/8 teaspoon ground black pepper

Directions
- Switch on the oven, then set it to 350 degrees F and let it preheat.
- Separate egg whites and yolks between two bowls, and then beat the egg whites until stiff peaks form.
- Add bacon, fold until mixed, scoop the mixture into two mounds onto a baking sheet lined with parchment paper.
- Make a small well in the middle of each mound by using a small bowl, bake for 3 minutes, then add an egg yolk into each well and continue baking for 2 minutes.
- Season eggs with salt and black pepper and then serve.

Lunch – Bacon and Cauliflower Mac and Cheese

Serving: 2
Preparation time: 5 minutes; Cooking time: 20 minutes
Nutritional Info: 152.5 Cal; 14 g Fats; 2 g Protein; 1.5 g Net Carb; 0.25 g Fiber;
Ingredients
- 2 strips of bacon

- ½ cup cauliflower florets, chopped
- 3 tablespoons butter, unsalted
- 3 ounces whipped topping
- 3 tablespoons grated cheddar cheese

Extra:

- ½ teaspoon salt
- 1/8 teaspoon ground black pepper
- ¼ teaspoon cayenne pepper
- ¾ cup of water

Directions

- Take a skillet pan, place it over medium heat and when hot, add bacon and cook for 5 minutes or until crispy.
- Transfer bacon to a plate, pat dry with paper towels, chop the bacon and set aside until required.
- Take a saucepan, place it over medium heat, pour in water, bring to boil, then add cauliflower florets and boil for 4 minutes.
- When done, drain the cauliflower and then set aside until required.
- Return saucepan over medium heat, add butter, whipped topping, salt, black pepper, and cayenne pepper, cook for 3 to 5 minutes until the butter has melted and a thick sauce comes together, stirring continuously.
- Then add cauliflower florets in it, stir well until combined, sprinkle with cheese, and stir until cheese has melted.
- Add bacon into the sauce, stir until combined, and remove the pan from heat.
- Serve straight away.

Dinner – Turkey Sesame Coleslaw

Serving: 2
Preparation time: 5 minutes; Cooking time: 13 minutes
Nutritional Info: 117.5 Cal; 8.4 g Fats; 8 g Protein; 1.8 g Net Carb; 1 g Fiber;
Ingredients

- 4 ounces ground turkey
- 6 ounces coleslaw
- 1 tablespoon sesame oil
- 1 tablespoon fish sauce

Directions

- Take a skillet pan, place it over medium heat, add turkey, drizzle with sesame oil and fish sauce and cook for 5 to 8 minutes until turkey has thoroughly cooked.

- Add coleslaw, toss until mixed, and then cook for 3 minutes until softened.
- Serve straight away.

Day 7
Breakfast – Cauliflower and Bacon Hash

Serving: 2
Preparation time: 5 minutes; Cooking time: 15 minutes
Nutritional Info: 211.5 Cal; 18.6 g Fats; 9 g Protein; 1.3 g Net Carb; 0.3 g Fiber;
Ingredients
- ½ cup chopped cauliflower florets
- 2 slices of bacon, diced
- ¼ teaspoon paprika
- 1 tablespoon olive oil

Extra:
- 1/3 teaspoon salt
- 1/8 teaspoon ground black pepper
- 1 ½ tablespoon water

Directions
- Take a skillet pan, place it over medium-high heat, add bacon, and cook for 3 to 5 minutes until crispy.
- Transfer bacon to a plate, then add cauliflower into the pan and cook for 3 minutes until golden.
- Season with salt, black pepper, and paprika, drizzle with water, and cook for 3 to 5 minutes until cauliflower has softened.
- Chop the bacon, add it into the pan, stir well, cook for 2 minutes and then remove the pan from heat.
- Serve straight away.

Lunch – Lemon Garlic Roasted Brussels sprouts

Serving: 2
Preparation time: 5 minutes; Cooking time15 6 minutes
Nutritional Info: 145 Cal; 13.4 g Fats; 1.1 g Protein; 2.8 g Net Carb; 2.3 g Fiber;

Ingredients
- 3 ounces Brussel sprouts, halved
- 2 tablespoons olive oil
- ¼ teaspoon garlic powder
- ½ of a lemon, juiced

Extra:
- 1/3 teaspoon salt
- ¼ teaspoon ground black pepper

Directions
- Switch on the oven, then set it to 400 degrees F and let it preheat.
- Meanwhile, take a sheet pan, line it with parchment sheet, place Brussel sprout halves on it and drizzle with oil and lemon juice.
- Season Brussel sprouts with garlic powder, salt, and black pepper, toss until well mixed and cook for 10 to 15 minutes until done, tossing halfway through.
- Serve straight away.

Dinner – BBQ Chicken Tender

Serving: 2
Preparation time: 5 minutes; Cooking time: 14 minutes
Nutritional Info: 196 Cal; 12.6 g Fats; 14.7 g Protein; 2.9 g Net Carb; 3 g Fiber;
Ingredients
- 2 chicken thighs, boneless
- 4 tablespoons chopped almond
- 1/3 cup low-carb BBQ sauce
- 1 tablespoon olive oil

Directions
- Switch on the oven, then set it to 375 degrees F and let it preheat.
- Meanwhile, cut chicken into strips, then coat it with BBQ sauce and dredge with chopped almonds.
- Take a baking sheet, line it with parchment paper, place prepared chicken tenders on it, then drizzle with oil and cook for 7 minutes.
- Brush BBQ on both sides of chicken tender, continue cooking for 5 to 7 minutes, and then serve.

Chapter 8

Recipes

WEEK 1

Shopping List

Look in pantry for:
- Unsalted butter
- Coconut oil
- Sesame oil
- Himalayan pink salt/sea salt
- Organic black pepper
- Organic cumin
- Organic red chili powder
- Organic dried basil
- Organic dried oregano
- Organic cayenne pepper
- Organic curry powder
- Organic garlic powder
- Soy sauce, low-sodium
- Apple cider vinegar

Purchase the following:

Items:	Store:	Quantity:	Price:
Large white eggs, 12 count, 24 oz.	Walmart Grocery	12	1.07
Broccoli florets, 32 oz.	Walmart Grocery	1	1.76
Iceberg lettuce	Walmart Grocery	1	1.28
Organic Hass avocados, count 5	Walmart Grocery	1	2.42
Ground turkey roll, 1 pound	Walmart Grocery	1	2.32
Shredded mild cheddar cheese, 8 oz.	Walmart Grocery	1	1.74
Whipped topping, 8 oz.	Walmart Grocery	1	0.72
Dry roasted & unsalted peanuts, 4 oz.	Walmart Grocery	1	0.48
Chicken thighs, 6-8 per pack	Kroger	1	2.44

Turkey bacon, 12 oz.	Amazon Fresh	1	2.08
Organic zucchini squash, 1.5 lb., 5 count	Amazon Fresh	1	3.27
Tomato sauce with roasted garlic, keto-friendly, 8 oz.	Amazon Fresh	1	0.46
		Total:	19.86

Day 1
Breakfast – Scrambled Eggs

Serving: 2
Nutritional Info: 163.5 Cal; 15.5 g Fats; 5.5 g Protein; 0.5 g Net Carb
Ingredients
- 1-ounce unsalted butter
- 2 large eggs, pasteurized
- 1/8 teaspoon salt
- 1/8 teaspoon cracked black pepper

Directions
- Take a medium bowl, crack the eggs in it and whisk them with a fork until frothy, and then season with salt and black pepper.
- Take a medium skillet pan, place it over medium heat, add butter and when it melts, pour in eggs and cook for 2 minutes until creamy, stirring continuously.
- Divide the eggs evenly between two plates and serve.

Lunch – Ground Turkey Stuffed Zucchini Boats

Serving: 2, Nutritional Info: 291 Cal; 22 g Fats; 14.5 g Protein; 5.5 g Net Carb; 1.5 g
Ingredients
- 1 medium zucchini
- 0.25-pounds ground turkey
- ½ cup tomato sauce
- ½ cup grated cheddar cheese
- 1 tablespoon coconut oil, melted

Extra:
- ½ teaspoon of sea salt
- ½ teaspoon garlic power
- ½ teaspoon Italian seasoning

Directions
- Switch on the oven, then set it to 400 degrees F and let it preheat.
- Meanwhile, cut the zucchini in half lengthwise and then create a well by scooping out some center with a spoon.
- Take a medium baking sheet, line it with aluminum foil, place zucchini halved on it, drizzle with ½ tablespoon oil, season with ¼ teaspoon salt, and roast for 15 to 20 minutes until softened.

- Meanwhile, take a skillet pan, place it over medium heat, add remaining oil and when hot, add ground turkey and cook for 7 to 10 minutes or until nicely browned.
- Sprinkle garlic and salt over turkey and continue cooking for 1 minute until fragrant, remove the pan from heat.
- Pour in tomato sauce, season with Italian seasoning, add 1/3 cup cheese and stir well.
- When zucchini halves have roasted, pat them dry with paper towels and stuff the wells with prepared meat mixture.
- Sprinkle remaining cheese on top and continue baking for 5 minutes until cheese has melted and turned golden-brown.

Dinner – Chicken and Peanut Stir-Fry

Serving: 2, Nutritional Info: 266 Cal; 19 g Fats; 18.5 g Protein; 4 g Net Carb; 2.5 g Fiber;
Ingredients
- 2 chicken thighs, cubed
- ½ cup broccoli florets
- ¼ cup peanuts
- 1 tablespoon sesame oil
- 1 ½ tablespoon soy sauce

Extra:
- ½ teaspoon garlic powder

Directions
- Take a skillet pan, place it over medium heat, add ½ tablespoon oil and when hot, add chicken cubes and cook for 4 minutes until browned on all sides.
- Then add broccoli florets and continue cooking for 2 minutes until tender-crisp. Add remaining ingredients, stir well and cook for another two months.
- Serve straight away.

Day 2
Breakfast – Egg Muffin

Serving: 2; Nutritional Info: 68.5 Cal; 27 g Fats; 3 g Protein; 0.5 g Ingredients
- 2 large eggs

- ¼ teaspoon of sea salt
- 1/8 teaspoon cracked black pepper
- 1/8 teaspoon dried thyme
- 1/8 teaspoon garlic powder

Directions

- Switch on the oven, then set it to 400 degrees F, and let preheat. Take a medium bowl, crack eggs in it, add remaining ingredients, and then whisk until well blended.
- Take two silicone muffin cups, line them with muffin liners, and evenly pour in egg mixture.
- Bake the muffins for 10 to 12 minutes until muffins have set, and the top is nicely golden brown and then take out muffins from the silicone cups.

Lunch – Cobb salad

Serving: 1

Nutritional Info: 206 Cal; 11.8 g Fats; 19.2 g Protein; 6 g Net Carb; 3 g Fiber;

Ingredients

- 1 large egg, hard-boiled, peeled, diced
- 2 ounces chicken thigh
- 2 1/2 slices bacon, cooked, crumbled
- ½ of a medium avocado, diced
- ½ cup chopped lettuce

Extra:

- 1 cup of water
- 3 tablespoon apple cider vinegar
- 1 ½ tablespoon coconut oil
- ¼ teaspoon salt
- 1/8 teaspoon ground black pepper

Directions

- Cook chicken thigh and for this, place chicken thighs in an instant pot, pour in 1 cup water, and shut the pot with a lid.
- Cook the chicken for 5 minutes at high pressure, and when done, let the pressure release naturally.
- Meanwhile, cook the bacon and for this, take a skillet pan, place it over medium heat and when hot, add bacon slices.
- Cook the bacon for 3 to 5 minutes until golden brown, then transfer them to a cutting board and chop the bacon, reserve the bacon grease in the pan for the next meal.
- When chicken thigh has cooked, transfer it to a bowl and shred the chicken with two forks, reserving the chicken broth for later use.
- Assemble the salad and for this, place lettuce in a salad plate, top with chicken, bacon, diced eggs, avocado, and chicken in horizontal rows.
- Prepare the dressing and for this, whisk together salt, black pepper, vinegar, and oil until incorporated and then drizzle the dressing generously over the salad.
- Serve straight away.

Dinner – Meaty Zucchini Noodles

Serving: 2; Nutritional Info: 229 Cal; 17 g Fats; 15 g Protein; 2 g

Ingredients
- 1 medium zucchini
- 1/2 pound ground turkey
- ¼ Tsp dried oregano
- ¼ teaspoon garlic powder
- ½ teaspoon curry powder

Extra:
- ½ teaspoon salt
- ½ teaspoon ground black pepper

Directions
- Prepare zucchini noodles, and for this, cut off the bottom and top of zucchini and then use a spiralizer to convert into noodles, set aside until required.
- Return the skillet pan with bacon grease over medium-high heat, add ground beef, stir well and cook for 5 minutes until meat is no longer pink.
- Season with oregano, garlic powder, curry powder, salt, and black pepper and cook for 5 to 7 minutes until turkey has cooked through.
- Then add zucchini noodles, toss until well mixed, and continue cooking 5 minutes until noodles have cooked to desired doneness.

Day 3
Breakfast – Salad sandwiches

Serving: 2

Nutritional Info: 187 Cal; 17 g Fats; 5 g Protein; 4 g Net Carb; 1.5 g Fiber;

Ingredients
- 1 medium avocado, peeled, pitted, diced
- 2 leaves of iceberg lettuce
- 1-ounce unsalted butter
- 2-ounce cheddar cheese, sliced

Directions
- Rinse the lettuce leaves, pat dry with a paper towel, and then smear each leaf with butter.
- Top lettuce with cheese and avocado and serve.

Lunch – Shredded Chicken in a lettuce wrap

Serving: 2
Nutritional Info: 143.5 Cal; 1.4 g Fats; 21.7 g Protein; 3.4 g Net Carb; 0.7 g Fiber;
Ingredients

- 2 leaves of iceberg lettuce
- 2 large chicken thigh
- 2 tablespoon shredded cheddar cheese
- 3 cups hot water
- 4 tablespoon tomato sauce

Extra:
- 1 tablespoon soy sauce
- 1 tablespoon red chili powder
- ¾ teaspoon salt
- ½ teaspoon cracked black pepper

Directions
- Switch on the instant pot, place chicken thighs in it, and add remaining ingredients except for lettuce.
- Stir until just mixed, shut the instant pot with a lid and cook for 15 minutes at high pressure and when done, release the pressure naturally.
- Then open the instant pot, transfer chicken to a cutting board and shred with two forks.
- Evenly divide the chicken between two lettuce leaves, and drizzle with some of the cooking liquid, reserving the remaining cooking liquid for later use as chicken broth.
- Serve straight away.

Dinner – Broccoli and Cheese Soup

Serving: 2; Nutritional Info: 145.5 Cal; 12.5 g Fats; 6.5 g Protein; 2 g Net Carb; 0.5 g Fiber;

Ingredients
- ¾ cup broccoli florets
- ½ teaspoon garlic powder
- ½ cup shredded cheddar cheese
- ¼ cup whipped topping

- 1 cup chicken broth, reserved

Extra:
- ½ teaspoon salt
- ½ teaspoon cracked black pepper

Directions
- Take a large pot, place it over medium heat, pour in reserved chicken broth, and stir in whipped topping.
- Add broccoli florets, season with salt and black pepper and cook for 10 minutes until florets are tender.
- Remove the pot from heat and use an immersion blender to puree the soup until smooth.
- Then return the pot to low heat, add ¼ cup cheese, stir until it melts, then add remaining cheese and stir until it melts.
- Ladle soup into bowls and serve.

Day 4
Breakfast – Bacon, and Eggs

Serving: 2; Nutritional Info: 136 Cal; 11 g Fats; 7.5 g Protein; 1 g Net Carb; 0 g Fiber;
Ingredients
- 2 eggs
- 4 slices of turkey bacon
- ¼ teaspoon salt
- ¼ teaspoon ground black pepper

Directions
- Take a skillet pan, place it over medium heat, add bacon slices in it and cook for 5 minutes until crispy.
- Transfer bacon slices to a plate and set aside until required, reserving the fat in the pan.
- Cook the egg in the pan one at a time, and for this, crack an egg in the pan and cook for 2 to 3 minutes or more until the egg has cooked to desire level.
- Transfer egg to a plate and cook the other egg in the same manner.
- Season eggs with salt and black pepper and then serve with cooked bacon.

Lunch – Turkey Lettuce Wraps

Serving: 2; Nutritional Info: 210 Cal; 17 g Fats; 10 g Protein; 2.5 g
Ingredients
- ¼ pound ground turkey
- 2 leaves of iceberg lettuce
- 1 tablespoon sesame oil
- 2 tablespoons soy sauce
- 1 tbsp cheddar cheese

Extra:
- 1 teaspoon garlic powder
- 1 teaspoon coconut oil
- ¼ teaspoon salt
- ¼ tsp cracked black pepper

Directions
- Take a skillet pan, place it over medium heat, add coconut oil and when hot, add turkey and cook for 7 to 10 minutes until nicely browned.
- Meanwhile, rinse the leaves of lettuce and pat dry with a paper towel, set aside until required.
- Prepare the sauce, and for this, whisk together sesame oil, soy sauce, garlic powder, salt, and black pepper.

- Pour the sauce into the cooked turkey and continue cooking for 3 minutes or until the sauce has evaporated.
- Evenly divide the meat between two lettuce leaves, top with cheddar cheese, wrap it and serve.

Dinner – Stir-Fried Zucchini and Turkey

Serving: 2; Nutritional Info: 82 Cal; 5.6 g Fats; 5.2 g Protein; 2.4 g Net Carb; 1.3 g Fiber;

Ingredients

- 1 large zucchini, sliced
- ¼ pound ground turkey
- 3 tablespoons shredded cheddar cheese
- 1 teaspoon soy sauce

Extra:

- 2/3 teaspoon salt, divided
- ¼ teaspoon red chili pepper
- ½ teaspoon ground black pepper

Directions

- Take a skillet pan, place it over high heat and when hot, add ¾ teaspoon oil and turkey, season with 1/3 teaspoon salt and black pepper and cook for 3 to 5 minutes until stir-fried.
- Transfer turkey to a plate, add zucchini slices into the pan, drizzle with soy sauce and sesame oil, and salt, stir well, and cook for 2 minutes until zucchini has almost cooked.
- Return turkey into the pan, toss well until mixed, and then remove the pan from heat.
- Evenly divide turkey and zucchini between two plates, top evenly with cheese and serve.

Day 5
Breakfast – Boiled Eggs

Serving: 2; Nutritional Info: 112 Cal; 9.5 g Fats; 5.5 g Protein; 1 g Net Carb; 0 g Fiber;
Ingredients
- 2 eggs
- ½ of a medium avocado

Extra:
- ¼ teaspoon salt
- ¼ teaspoon ground black pepper

Directions
- Place a medium pot over medium heat, fill it half full with water and bring it to boil.
- Then carefully place the eggs in the boiling water and boil the eggs for 5 minutes until soft-boiled, 8 minutes for medium-boiled, and 10 minutes for hard-boiled.
- When eggs have boiled, transfer them to a bowl containing chilled water and let them rest for 5 minutes.
- Then crack the eggs with a spoon and peel them.
- Cut each egg into slices, season with salt and black pepper, and serve with diced avocado.

Lunch – Buttery Broccoli and Bacon

Serving: 2; Nutritional Info: 77 Cal; 5 g Fats; 5 g Protein; 1 g Net Carb
Ingredients
- 1 slice of turkey bacon
- 1 cup chopped broccoli florets
- 1/8 teaspoon garlic powder
- ¼ teaspoon Italian seasoning
- ¼ tablespoon unsalted butter

Extra:
- 1/8 teaspoon salt
- 1/8 teaspoon ground black pepper

Directions
- Take a medium skillet pan, place it over high heat, add bacon slice and cook for 3 to 5 minutes until crispy.
- Transfer bacon to a cutting board and then chop it into small pieces.
- Reduce the heat to medium-low level, add broccoli florets into the pan, stir well into the bacon grease, add butter, then toss until mixed and cook for 5 minutes until tender.
- Season the broccoli florets with salt, black pepper, and Italian seasoning, add chopped bacon, stir well and cook for 2 minutes until thoroughly heated.

Dinner – Garlic Cheddar Chicken Thighs

Serving: 2; Nutritional Info: 128.5 Cal; 9.5 g Fats; 9 g Protein; 0.2 g Carb

Ingredients

- 2 chicken thighs
- 1/3 teaspoon garlic powder
- 1/3 tablespoon dried basil
- 1/3 tablespoon grated cheddar cheese
- ½ teaspoon coconut oil

Extra:

- 1/8 teaspoon salt
- 1/3 teaspoon ground black pepper

Directions

- Switch on the oven, then set it to 450 degrees F, and let preheat.
- Meanwhile, prepare the herb mix and for this, stir together ¼ teaspoon oil, salt, black pepper, cheese, and basil until combined.
- Create a pocket into each chicken thigh and then stuff it with half of the prepared herb mix and spread the remaining herb mix evenly on chicken thighs.
- Take a skillet pan, place it over medium-high heat, add remaining oil and when hot, place stuffed chicken thighs in it and cook for 4 minutes.
- Then flip the chicken thighs, cook for 5 to 7 minutes until chicken is no longer pink and then roast the chicken thighs for 10 to 12 minutes until a meat thermometer inserted into the thickest part of thighs read 160 degrees F.
- Let chicken thighs rest for 5 minutes and then serve.

Day 6
Breakfast – Breakfast Patties

Serving: 2; Nutritional Info: 154.5 Cal; 8.5 g Fats; 15.5 g Protein; 4 g Net Carb; 4 g Fiber;
Ingredients

- ½ pound ground turkey
- ½ teaspoon garlic powder
- 1/2 teaspoon smoked paprika
- 1 tablespoon coconut oil
- 2 leaves of iceberg lettuce

Extra:
- 1/2 teaspoon dried thyme
- ½ teaspoon salt
- 1/4 teaspoon ground black pepper

Directions
- Take a medium bowl, place ground turkey in it, and then add remaining ingredients except for oil.
- Stir well until combined and then shape the mixture into two patties.
- Take a skillet pan, place it over medium heat, add oil and when hot, add patties and cook for 4 to 5 minutes per side until nicely browned and thoroughly cooked.
- Wrap each patty in a lettuce leaf and serve.

Lunch – Broccoli Salad with Bacon

Serving: 2
Nutritional Info: 119 Cal; 10 g Fats; 3.5 g Protein; 2 g Net Carb; 0.5 g Fiber;
Ingredients
- 1 cup broccoli florets, chopped
- 4 tablespoons whipped topping
- 2 tablespoons shredded cheddar cheese
- 3 slices of turkey bacon, cooked, chopped
- 1/3 teaspoon garlic powder

Extra:
- 1/8 teaspoon salt
- 1/8 teaspoon dried parsley

Directions
- Take a medium bowl, place whipped topping in it, whisk in garlic powder and parsley, and then fold in broccoli florets.
- Top with bacon and cheddar cheese and serve.

Dinner – Casserole with Turkey and Broccoli

Serving: 2; Nutritional Info: 323 Cal; 27.5 g Fats; 16.5 g Protein; 2.5 g Net Carb; 1.5 g Fiber;

Ingredients
- 4-ounce broccoli florets
- ½ pound ground turkey
- 2-ounce unsalted butter
- ¼ cup shredded cheddar cheese

Extra:
- 1/3 teaspoon salt
- 1/8 teaspoon cracked black pepper

Directions
- Take a medium skillet pan, place it over medium-high heat, add butter and when it melted, add turkey and broccoli and cook for 5 to 7 minutes until beef has thoroughly cooked.
- Season beef and broccoli with salt and black pepper, then reduce heat to a low level and continue cooking for 3 to 5 minutes or until broccoli has fried.
- Remove pan from heat, transfer beef and broccoli to a casserole, sprinkle cheese on top and broil for 3 minutes, or until cheese melts.
- Serve straight away.

Day 7
Breakfast – Bacon and Egg Fat Bombs

Serving: 2, Nutritional Info: 92.5 Cal; 9.2 g Fats; 2.5 g Protein; 0.1 g Net Carb; 0.6 g
Ingredients
- 2 slices of turkey bacon
- 1 large egg, hard-boiled
- 2 tablespoons unsalted butter, softened
- 1 tablespoon whipped topping
- ¾ teaspoon grated cheddar cheese

Extra:
- ¼ teaspoon salt
- ¼ teaspoon ground black pepper

Directions
- Switch on the oven, then set it to 375 degrees F, and let preheat.
- Then take a baking sheet, line it with parchment paper, place bacon slices on it and cook for 10 minutes until nicely golden brown.
- Meanwhile, boil the egg and for this, place a medium pot half-full with water over medium heat and bring to boil.
- Then add egg and cook for 10 minutes until hard-boiled.
- Transfer the egg in a bowl containing chilled water, let it rest for 5 minutes, and then peel it. Chop the egg, then place it in a bowl, season with salt and black pepper, add whipped topping and cheese, stir until well combined, and refrigerate for 15 minutes until solid.
- Crumble the roasted bacon into small pieces and then place it in a shallow dish.
- Remove the solid egg mixture from the refrigerator and shape the mixture into two large balls. Roll the egg balls into crumbled bacon until evenly coated, then place the ball on a plate and store the balls for up to 5 days in the refrigerator.
- When ready to serve, let the balls rest for some time at room temperature until slightly softened and then serve.

Lunch – Taco Stuffed Avocados

Serving:2; Nutritional Info: 210 Cal; 16 g Fats; 13 g Protein; 2 g Net Carb; 1.5 g Fiber;
Ingredients
- ¼ pound ground turkey
- 2-ounce tomato sauce
- 1 medium avocado, pitted, halved
- ½ cup shredded cheddar cheese
- 2 tablespoon shredded lettuce

Extra:
- 1/8 teaspoon garlic powder
- ¼ teaspoon salt
- ½ tablespoon red chili powder

Directions
- Take a skillet pan, place it over medium heat, add ground turkey and cook for 5 minutes until nicely golden brown.
- Reserve the grease for later use, then season the turkey with garlic powder, salt, and red chili powder, stir in tomato sauce and cook for 3 minutes until meat has thoroughly cooked.
- Cut avocado into half, remove its pit and then stuff the crater with prepared meat.
- Top meat with cheddar cheese and lettuce and serve.

Dinner – Zucchini Noodle Carbonara

Serving:2; Nutritional Info: 114 Cal; 7 g Fats; 8 g Protein; 1.5 g Net Carb

Ingredients
- 2 large zucchini
- 1 large egg
- 1 egg yolk
- ¼ cup grated cheddar cheese
- 3 slices of turkey bacon, diced

Extra:
- 1/4 teaspoon sea salt
- 1/2 teaspoon fresh ground black pepper

Directions
- Prepare zucchini noodles, and for this, cut off the bottom and top of zucchini and then use a spiralizer to convert into noodles.
- Take a baking sheet, line it with a paper towel, then lay the zucchini noodles on them, sprinkle with salt, and let sit for 5 minutes. Then wrap zucchini noodles in a cheesecloth and squeeze well to remove its liquid as much as possible and set aside until required.
- Prepare the sauce and for this, crack the egg in a bowl, add egg yolk and cheese and whisk until well combined.
- Take a skillet pan, place it over medium heat, add bacon slices, and cook for 3 to 5 minutes until crispy.
- Then add zucchini noodles and cook for 3 minutes until warmed through.
- Switch heat to a low level, pour in egg mixture, stir well and remove the pan from heat.
- Stir the zucchini noodle until the egg is just cooked and then sprinkle with black pepper
- Serve straight away.

Shopping List for Week 2

Remaining foods from the previous week(s):

- Turkey bacon slices
- 2 avocados
- Iceberg lettuce
- Whipped topping
- Peanuts
- 1½ cup chicken broth

Look in pantry for:

- Himalayan pink salt/sea salt
- Organic black pepper
- Organic garlic powder
- Organic cayenne pepper
- Organic red pepper flakes
- Organic Italian seasoning
- Organic dried basil
- Organic dried thyme
- Coconut oil
- Sesame oil
- Soy sauce, low-sodium
- Mustard

Purchase the following:

Items:	Store:	Quantity:	Price:
Large white eggs, 12 count, 24 oz.	Walmart Grocery	1	1.07
Cauliflower florets, 12 oz.	Walmart Grocery	1	1
Turkey roll, 16 oz.	Walmart Grocery	1	2.45
Zucchini, green	Walmart Grocery	1	0.82
Fresh spinach, 12 oz.	Walmart Grocery	1	0.93
Green onion bunch	Walmart Grocery	1	0.71
Tuna In Water, 5 oz.	Walmart Grocery	2	1.86
Cut Green Beans, 14.5 oz.	Walmart Grocery	1	0.47

Lemon	Walmart Grocery	1	0.45
Porkchop, center-cut, boneless	Walmart Grocery	1	2.32
Shredded Italian styled parmesan cheese, 8 oz.	Walmart Grocery	1	1.74
Italian basil pesto	Walmart Grocery	1	2.26
Fresh parsley bunch	Walmart Grocery	1	0.48
Fresh cilantro bunch	Walmart Grocery	1	0.48
Chicken thighs, 6-8 per pack	Kroger	1	2.44
		Total:	19.48

Day 8
Breakfast – Bacon and Egg Breakfast Muffin

Serving: 2; Nutritional Info: 78 Cal; 5.3 g Fats; 6.1 g Protein; 0.1 g Carb
Ingredients
- 2 slices of turkey bacon
- 2 large eggs
- ½ tablespoon chopped parsley
- ½ tablespoon chopped green onion
- 1 tablespoon whipped topping

Directions
- Switch on the oven, then set it to 375 degrees F, and let preheat.
- Take a skillet pan, place it over medium heat and when hot, add bacon and cook for 3 to 5 minutes until crispy.
- Transfer bacon to a cutting board and then chop it, reserving the grease in the pan.
- Crack the eggs in a bowl, whisk until blended, then add chopped bacon, green onion and whipped topping and stir until well combined.
- Take two silicone muffin cups, coat them with bacon grease, then evenly fill with the prepared mixture and bake for 15 to 20 minutes or until the edges of muffins are golden brown.

Lunch – Tuna Cakes

Serving: 2; Nutritional Info: 111.5 Cal; 7.5 g Fats; 9.5 g Protein; 0.4 g Net Carb; 0.1 g Fiber;
Ingredients
- 5-ounce tuna, packed in water
- 1 tablespoon mustard
- 1 teaspoon garlic powder
- 1 tablespoon coconut oil

Extra:
- ¼ teaspoon salt
- 1/8 teaspoon ground black pepper

Directions
- Drain the tuna, add it in a medium bowl and break it well with a fork.
- Then add remaining ingredients, stir until well mixed and then shape the mixture into four patties.
- Take a medium skillet pan, place it over medium heat, add oil and when hot, add tuna patties and cook for 3 minutes per side until golden brown.
- Serve patties straight away or serve as a wrap with iceberg lettuce.

Dinner – Pork Chops with Thyme

Serving:
Nutritional Info: 363 Cal; 23 g Fats; 34 g Protein; 3 g Net Carb; 2 g Fiber;
Ingredients
- ½ pound pork chops, about 4
- ½ of a lemon, cut into wedges
- 1 teaspoon dried thyme
- ¾ tablespoon unsalted butter, diced

Extra:
- 2 ½ teaspoons coconut oil, divided
- 1 teaspoon salt
- 1 teaspoon ground black pepper

Directions
- Switch on the oven, then set it to 350 degrees F, and let preheat.
- Meanwhile, place pork chops on clean working space, brush the exposed side with ¾ teaspoon oil, then sprinkle with ½ teaspoon salt, black pepper, and thyme and gently massage into the meat.
- Take a small skillet pan, place it over high heat, add ½ tablespoon oil and when hot, add a pork chop in it, seasoned side down, then drizzle with ¼ teaspoon olive, sprinkle with 1/8 teaspoon each of salt, black pepper and thyme and cook for 2 minutes per side until seared.
- Take a sheet pan, grease it with oil, place seared pork chops on it, add lemon wedges, top with diced butter and bake for 25 minutes or until a meat thermometer inserted into the thickest part of the chop reads 145 degrees F.
- Serve pork chops with roasted lemon.

Day 9
Breakfast – Egg Butter

Serving: 2; Nutritional Info: 159 Cal; 16.5 g Fats; 3 g Protein; 0.2 g Net Carb; 0 g Fiber;

Ingredients
- 2 large eggs, hard-boiled
- 3-ounce unsalted butter
- ½ teaspoon dried oregano
- ½ teaspoon dried basil
- 2 leaves of iceberg lettuce

Extra:
- ½ teaspoon of sea salt
- ¼ teaspoon ground black pepper

Directions
- Peel the eggs, then chop them finely and place in a medium bowl.
- Add remaining ingredients and stir well.
- Serve egg butter wrapped in a lettuce leaf.

Lunch – Roasted Green Beans

Serving: 2; Nutritional Info: 119 Cal; 9 g Fats; 5 g Protein; 4.5 g Net Carb; 3 g Fiber;

Ingredients
- ½ pound green beans
- ½ cup grated parmesan cheese
- 3 tablespoons coconut oil
- ½ teaspoon garlic powder

Extra:
- 1/3 teaspoon salt
- 1/8 teaspoon ground black pepper

Directions
- Switch on the oven, then set it to 425 degrees F, and let preheat.
- Take a baking sheet, line green beans on it, and set aside until required.
- Prepare the dressing, and for this, place remaining ingredients in a bowl, except for cheese and whisk until combined.

- Drizzle the dressing over green beans, toss until well coated, and then bake for 20 minutes until green beans are tender-crisp.
- Then sprinkle cheese on top of beans and continue roasting for 3 to 5 minutes or until cheese melts and nicely golden brown.
- Serve straight away.

Dinner – Ground Turkey and Veggie Stir-Fry

Serving: 2; Nutritional Info: 183 Cal; 11 g Fats; 15 g Protein; 4 g Net Carb; 2 g Fiber;
Ingredients

- 0.25-ounce ground turkey
- ¼ cup spinach
- 1 large zucchini, diced
- 2 green onion, sliced
- 2 slices of bacon, cooked, crumbled

Extra:
- ¾ teaspoon garlic powder
- ¾ teaspoon cayenne pepper
- ½ teaspoon salt
- 1 tablespoon soy sauce

Directions

- Take a skillet pan, place it over medium-high heat, add bacon slices and cook for 5 minutes until crispy.
- When done, transfer bacon to a cutting board and set aside until required.
- Add zucchini and green onions into the pan, cook for 5 minutes until stir-fry, then transfer vegetables to a plate and set aside.
- Add ground turkey into the pan, season with ¼ teaspoon of salt, cook for 7 to 10 minutes until nicely browned, and then transfer to a bowl, set aside until required.
- Add spinach into the pan, cook for 3 minutes, or until leaves have wilted and then drain well into the colander.
- Return turkey, zucchini, and green onion into the pan, season with garlic powder, cayenne pepper, remaining salt, stir well, and cook for 1 minute until fragrant.
- Drizzle with soy sauce, toss until well coated, add spinach and bacon, stir well combined and cook for 1 minute until thoroughly heated.
- Serve straight away.

Day 10
Breakfast – Garlic Parmesan Bacon Knots

Serving: 2; Nutritional Info: 27 Cal; 2 g Fats; 2 g Protein; 0.5 g Net Carb; 0.5 g Fiber;
Ingredients
- 4 slices of turkey bacon
- ¼ teaspoon garlic powder
- ¼ teaspoon red pepper flakes
- ¼ teaspoon Italian seasoning
- 2 tablespoons grated parmesan cheese

Directions
- Switch on the oven, then set it to 425 degrees F, and let preheat.
- Working on a slice of bacon at a time, tie it into a double knot and then place it on a baking sheet.
- Prepare remaining bacon knots in the same manner, season evenly with garlic powder, red pepper, and Italian seasoning and then bake for 7 to 10 minutes until almost crisp.
- Then sprinkle cheese over bacon knots and continue baking for 3 to 4 minutes until cheese has melted.
- Serve straight away.

Lunch – Fried Cauliflower and Egg Rice

Serving: 2; Nutritional Info: 57 Cal; 4 g Fats; 3 g Protein; 1.7 g Net Carb; 0.5 g Fiber;
Ingredients
- 8-ounce cauliflower florets, riced
- 2 green onion, sliced
- 1 large egg, beaten
- 1 tablespoons soy sauce
- ½ teaspoon toasted sesame oil

Extra:
- 1 tablespoon coconut oil
- ½ teaspoon garlic powder

Directions
- Take a large skillet pan, place it over medium-high heat, add coconut oil and riced cauliflower, and cook for 5 minutes until softened.

- Then add green onions, stir well and cook for 3 minutes until onions are tender.
- Season with salt, sprinkle garlic over cauliflower, cook for 1 minute until fragrant, then pour in the egg, stir well and cook for 2 minutes until the egg has scrambled to desire level, stirring continuously.
- Drizzle with soy sauce and sesame oil and serve straight away.

Dinner – Cheese and Cauliflower Soup

Serving: 2; Nutritional Info: 123.5 Cal; 9.3 g Fats; 4.5 g Protein; 1.2 g Net Carb; 0.4 g Fiber;

Ingredients

- 4 ounce chopped cauliflower
- 2 slices of turkey bacon
- 1 ¾ tablespoon whipped topping
- 1 1/2 cups chicken broth
- 4-ounce shredded parmesan cheese

Extra:

- ½ teaspoon salt
- ½ teaspoon ground black pepper
- ¼ teaspoon garlic powder

Directions

- Take a medium pot, place it over medium-high heat, then add turkey bacon and cook for 5 minutes until crispy.
- Transfer bacon to a plate, crumble it and reserve the grease from the pot.
- Add cauliflower into the pot, pour in chicken broth, season with salt and black pepper, add garlic powder and bring the mixture to boil.
- Then lower heat to medium-low level and simmer cauliflower for 5 to 7 minutes until tender.
- Remove pot from the heat, puree the mixture with an immersion blender, then add cheese and whipped topping and stir until well combined.
- Ladle soup into bowls, top with bacon and serve.

Day 11
Breakfast – Spinach Egg Muffins

Serving: 2; Nutritional Info: 55 Cal; 3.5 g Fats; 4.5 g Protein; 0.4 g Net Carb; 0.2 g Fiber;
Ingredients
- ½ cups chopped spinach
- 1/8 teaspoon dried basil
- 1/8 teaspoon garlic powder
- 2 large eggs
- 3 tablespoons grated Parmesan cheese

Extra:
- ¼ teaspoon of sea salt
- 1/8 teaspoon ground black pepper

Directions
- Switch on the oven, then set it to 400 degrees F, and let preheat.
- Meanwhile, place eggs in a bowl, season with salt and black pepper and whisk until blended.
- Add garlic and basil, whisk in mixed and then stir in spinach and cheese until combined.
- Take two silicone muffin cups, grease them with reserved bacon greased, fill them evenly with prepared egg mixture and bake for 8 to 10 minutes until the top has nicely browned.
- Serve straight away.

Lunch – Cheeseburger

Serving: 2; Nutritional Info: 203 Cal; 17.5 g Fats; 8.8 g Protein; 1.3 g Net Carb; 1 g Fiber;
Ingredients
- ½ pound ground turkey
- 2 slices of turkey bacon, cooked, crumbled
- 2-ounce shredded parmesan cheese, divided
- 2 tablespoons basil pesto
- 2 leaf of iceberg lettuce

Extra:
- 1 teaspoon dried oregano
- 1 tablespoon mustard
- ½ teaspoon salt
- 1 teaspoon garlic powder
- 1 teaspoon paprika powder

Directions
- Take a bowl, place ground turkey in it, add oregano, mustard, salt, garlic powder, paprika, mustard, and half of the cheese, stir until well mixed, and shape the mixture into two patties.

- Place a medium skillet pan over medium heat, add bacon and cook for 5 minutes until crispy, set aside until required.
- Add patties into the pan, cook for 4 to 5 minutes until the bottom has turned brown, then flip the patties, top each patty with remaining cheese and continue cooking for 4 minutes until done.
- Serve each patty on a lettuce leaf, top it with bacon and 1 tablespoon pesto, wrap it and serve.

Dinner – Tuna Stuffed Avocado

Serving: 2; Nutritional Info: 108.5 Cal; 8 g Fats; 6 g Protein; 0.8 g Net Carb; 2.3 g Fiber;

Ingredients

- 1 medium avocado
- ¼ of a lemon, juiced
- 5-ounce tuna, packed in water
- 1 green onion, chopped
- 2 slices of turkey bacon, cooked, crumbled

Extra:

- ¼ teaspoon salt
- ¼ teaspoon ground black pepper

Directions

- Drain tuna, place it in a bowl, and then broke it into pieces with a form.
- Add remaining ingredients, except for avocado and bacon, and stir until well combined.
- Cut avocado into half, remove its pit and then stuff its cavity evenly with the tuna mixture.
- Top stuffed avocados with bacon and serve straight away.

Day 12
Breakfast – Omelet

Serving: 2; Nutritional Info: 114.5 Cal; 9.3 g Fats; 4 g Protein; 1 g Net Carb; 0.2 g Fiber;
Ingredients
- 2 eggs
- 2 tablespoons shredded parmesan cheese, divided
- 1 tablespoon unsalted butter
- 2 slices of turkey bacon, diced

Extra:
- ¼ teaspoon salt
- 1/8 teaspoon ground black pepper

Directions
- Crack eggs in a bowl, add salt and black pepper, whisk well until fluffy and then whisk in 1 tablespoon cheese until combined.
- Take a medium skillet pan, add bacon slices on it, cook for 3 minutes until sauté, then pour in the egg mixture and cook for 4 minutes or until the omelet is almost firm.
- Lower heat to medium-low level, sprinkle remaining cheese on top of the omelet, then fold the omelet and cook for 1 minute.
- Slide the omelet to a plate, cut it in half, and serve immediately.

Lunch – Spinach Zucchini Boats

Serving: 2; Nutritional Info: 86.5 Cal; 6 g Fats; 4 g Protein; 3.5 g Net Carb; 0.5 g Fiber;
Ingredients
- 1 large zucchini
- ¾ cup spinach
- 1 ½ tablespoon whipped topping
- 3 tablespoons grated parmesan cheese
- ½ teaspoon garlic powder

Extra:
- ½ teaspoon salt
- ½ teaspoon ground black pepper

Directions
- Switch on the oven, then set it to 350 degrees F, and let preheat.
- Take a skillet pan, place it over medium heat, add spinach and cook for 5 to 7 minutes or until spinach leaves have wilted and their moisture has evaporated completely.

- Sprinkle garlic powder, ¼ teaspoon each of salt and black pepper over spinach, add whipped topping and 2 tablespoons cheese and stir well until the cheese has melted, remove the pan from heat.
- Cut off the top and bottom of zucchini, then cut it in half lengthwise and make a well by scooping out pulp along the center, leaving ½-inch shell.
- Season zucchini with remaining salt and black pepper, place them on a baking sheet and roast for 5 minutes.
- Then fill zucchini evenly with spinach mixture, top with remaining cheese and broil for 3 minutes until cheese has melted.
- Serve straight away.

Dinner – Chicken thighs with green beans

Serving: 2; Nutritional Info: 393 Cal; 33.5 g Fats; 20 g Protein; 4.1 g Net Carb; 0.5 g Fiber;

Ingredients

- 2 chicken thighs
- 6-ounce green beans
- ¼ of a lemon, juiced, zested
- 2-ounce unsalted butter
- 1 tablespoon coconut oil

Extra:

- ¾ teaspoon salt
- 1 teaspoon garlic powder
- 1 teaspoon dried basil
- 1 teaspoon dried thyme

Directions

- Prepare the chicken thighs, and for this, pat dry with paper towels and season with ½ teaspoon salt.
- Take a medium skillet pan, place it over medium heat, add oil and half of butter and when butter melt, add chicken thighs and cook for 5 minutes per side until thoroughly cooked.
- Meanwhile, prepare the sauce, and for this, whisk together lemon juice and zest, remaining salt, garlic, thyme, and oregano.
- Transfer cooked chicken thighs to a plate and set aside.
- Add green beans into the pan, cook them for 2 minutes, then pour in the sauce along with remaining butter, stir well until coated, and continue cooking for 2 minutes until beans have become tender-crisp.
- Increase heat to medium-high level, return chicken into the pan, and cook for 3 minutes.

Week 3

Shopping List for Week 3

Remaining foods from the previous week(s):
- Basil pesto
- Parsley bunch
- Cilantro bunch
- Green onion
- Peanuts

Look in pantry for:
- Organic garlic powder
- Organic minced garlic
- Himalayan pink salt/sea salt
- Organic black pepper
- Organic dried thyme
- Organic dried basil
- Organic Italian seasoning
- Organic lemon pepper seasoning
- Organic cinnamon
- Stevia
- Mayonnaise
- Soy sauce
- Apple cider vinegar
- Mustard
- Coconut oil
- Unsalted butter

Purchase the following:

Items:	Store:	Quantity:	Price:
Large white eggs, 12 count	Walmart	1	1.07
Broccoli Cuts, 32 oz.	Walmart	1	1.74
Shredded Cheddar Cheese, 8 oz.	Walmart	1	1.28
Green Beans, 14.5 oz.	Walmart	1	0.47
Roma Tomatoes	Walmart	3	0.42
Ground Turkey Roll, 16 ounces (1 pound)	Walmart	1	2.33
Zucchini, 2 count	Walmart	1	1.23
Turkey Bacon, 12 oz.	Walmart	1	2.28

Bone-In Chicken Thighs Family Pack, 4.75 - 5.25 lb	Walmart	1	5.35
Hass Avocados, each	Walmart	2	1.12
Lemon	Walmart	1	0.45
Celery	Walmart	1	1.38
		Total:	19.83

Day 15

Breakfast – Egg Salad

Serving: 2; Preparation time: 5 minutes; Cooking time: 0 minutes
Nutritional Info: 240.3 Cal; 22 g Fats; 10.8 g Protein; 0 g Net Carb; 0 g Fiber;
Ingredients
- 2 tablespoons mayonnaise
- 1 teaspoon lemon juice
- 2 large eggs, hard-boiled
- 2 slices of bacon, cooked, crumbled

Extra:
- 1/8 teaspoon cracked black pepper
- ¼ teaspoon salt

Directions
- Peel the eggs, then dice them and place them in a bowl.
- Add remaining ingredients except for bacon and stir until well mixed.
- Top with bacon and serve.

Lunch – Broccoli with Cheddar and Bacon

Serving: 2

Preparation time: 5 minutes; Cooking time: 30 minutes
Nutritional Info: 100 Cal; 100 g Fats; 100 g Protein; 100 g Net Carb; 100 g Fiber;
Ingredients

- 4 ounces broccoli florets
- 1/3 cup mayonnaise
- 1/3 cup grated cheddar cheese
- 2 ounces crumbled bacon
- 1 tablespoon coconut oil

Directions

1. Switch on the oven, then set it to 350 degrees F and let it preheat.
2. Then take a baking sheet, grease it with oil, spread broccoli florets on it and bake for 20 minutes until roasted.
3. Meanwhile, place mayonnaise in a bowl, add cheese, and stir until mixed.
4. When the broccoli has roasted, spread the mayonnaise-cheese mixture on top and continue baking for 10 minutes or until cheese is golden.

Dinner – Lemon Chicken Thighs

Serving: 2
Preparation time: 10 minutes; Cooking time: 10 minutes
Nutritional Info: 281.5 Cal; 19.1 g Fats; 26.7 g Protein; 0.3 g Net Carb; 0.4 g Fiber;
Ingredients

- 2 chicken thighs
- ½ teaspoon garlic powder
- ½ teaspoon dried thyme
- ½ of lemon, juiced, zested
- 1 cup of water

Extra:

- 2 tablespoons coconut oil
- ¼ teaspoon salt
- 1/8 teaspoon ground black pepper

Directions

1. Prepare spice rub and for this, stir together garlic, thyme, lemon zest, garlic, salt, and black pepper.
2. Prepare chicken and for this, brush chicken with oil and then season with the lemon-thyme mixture until evenly coated.
3. Switch on the instant pot, grease it with oil, press the saute button, and when hot, add seasoned chicken thighs and cook for 3 minutes per side until golden brown.
4. Then remove chicken thighs from the instant pot, pour in water, add lemon juice, and insert a trivet stand.

5. Place chicken on trivet stand, shut instant pot with lid, and cook at high pressure for 5 minutes.
6. When done, let quick pressure release, open the instant pot, and transfer chicken thighs to a plate, reserving the broth for later use.
7. Serve straight away.

Day 16

Breakfast – Bacon and Eggs Cups

Serving: 2; Preparation time: 10 minutes; Cooking time: 18 minutes
Nutritional Info: 67 Cal; 4 g Fats; 5 g Protein; 0 g Net Carb; 0 g Fiber;
Ingredients
- 2 eggs
- 2 slices of bacon

Extra:
- 1/4 teaspoon salt
- 1/4 teaspoon ground black pepper

Directions
1. Switch on the oven, then set it to 400 degrees F and let it preheat.
2. Then place bacon on a baking sheet, bake for 5 to 8 minutes until tender-crisp, and when done, cool bacon for 5 minutes and pat dry with paper towels.
3. Take two silicone muffin cups, grease them with oil, place a slice of bacon into each cup, wrapping it around the sides and then crack an egg into each cup.
4. Season egg with salt and black pepper and cook for 8 to 10 minutes until bacon has crispy and eggs have set.
5. Serve straight away.

Lunch – Cider Chicken

Serving: 2; Preparation time: 10 minutes; Cooking time: 18 minutes

Nutritional Info: 182.5 Cal; 107.5 g Fats; 15.5 g Protein; 2.5 g Net Carb; 0 g Fiber;

Ingredients

- 2 chicken thighs
- ¼ cup apple cider vinegar
- 1 teaspoon liquid stevia
- ½ tablespoon coconut oil
- 1/3 teaspoon salt
- ¼ teaspoon ground black pepper

Extra:

Directions

1. Switch on the oven, then set it to 450 degrees F and let it preheat.
2. Meanwhile, place chicken in a bowl, drizzle with oil and then season with salt and black pepper
3. Take a baking sheet, place prepared chicken thighs on it, and bake for 10 to 15 minutes or until its internal temperature reaches 165 degrees F.
4. In the meantime, take a small saucepan, place it over medium heat, pour in vinegar, stir in stevia and bring the mixture to boil.
5. Then switch heat to the low level and simmer sauce for 3 to 5 minutes until reduced by half, set aside until required.
6. When the chicken has roasted, brush it generously with prepared cider sauce, then switch on the broiler and bake the chicken for 3 minutes until golden brown.
7. Serve straight away.

Dinner – Avocado stuffed egg salad

Serving: 2

Preparation time: 10 minutes; Cooking time: 0 minutes

Nutritional Info: 131.8 Cal; 11.7 g Fats; 3.6 g Protein; 0.6 g Net Carb; 2.4 g Fiber;

Ingredients

- 2 tablespoons mayonnaise
- 2 large eggs, hard-boiled
- 1 green onion, chopped
- 1 avocado

Extra:

- 1/8 teaspoon ground black pepper
- ¼ teaspoon salt

Directions

1. Peel the eggs, then dice them and place them in a bowl.
2. Add remaining ingredients except for avocado and stir until well mixed.
3. Cut avocado in half, remove its pit, and then fill the avocado halved with prepared egg salad.
4. Serve straight away.

Day 17
Breakfast – Pesto Scramble

Serving: 2
Preparation time: 5 minutes; Cooking time: 5 minutes
Nutritional Info: 159.5 Cal; 14.5 g Fats; 7 g Protein; 0.4 g Net Carb; 0.1 g Fiber;
Ingredients

- 2 eggs
- 2 tablespoons grated cheddar cheese
- 1 tablespoon unsalted butter
- 1 tablespoon basil pesto

Extra:

- 1/8 teaspoon salt
- 1/8 teaspoon ground black pepper

Directions

1. Crack eggs in a bowl, add cheese, black pepper, salt, and pesto and whisk until combined.
2. Take a skillet pan, place it over medium heat, add butter and when it melts, pour in the egg mixture, and cook for 3 to 5 minutes until eggs have scrambled to the desired level.
3. Serve straight away.

Lunch – Slow Cooked Stuffed Tomatoes with Meat

Serving: 2
Preparation time: 10 minutes; Cooking time: 4 hours
Nutritional Info: 191.5 Cal; 12.6 g Fats; 16.3 g Protein; 2.3 g Net Carb; 1.1 g Fiber;
Ingredients

- 2 tomatoes
- 4 ounces ground turkey
- 1 tablespoon Italian seasoning
- 2 tablespoons grated cheddar cheese

Extra:
- ¼ teaspoon salt
- 1/8 teaspoon ground black pepper

Directions
1. Cut a thin slice from the top and end of tomatoes and then use a spoon to remove seeds of each tomato.
2. Mix together sausage, Italian seasoning, and salt and ground black pepper to taste, then fill this mixture evenly into tomatoes and sprinkle with cheese.
3. Grease a 4-quart slow cooker with a non-stick cooking spray and spread tomatoes with basil in the bottom and mix in 3/4 cup water.
4. Arrange stuffed tomatoes into the slow cooker, then cover and seal the slow cooker with its lid.
5. Plugin the slow cooker and adjust the cooking timer for 4 hours and let cook at high heat setting or until cooked.

Dinner – Broccoli and Bacon Stir-Fry

Serving: 2; Preparation time: 5 minutes; Cooking time: 15 minutes
Nutritional Info: 481 Cal; 38 g Fats; 30 g Protein; 2.7 g Net Carb; 2.1 g Fiber;
Ingredients
- 6-ounces broccoli florets, chopped
- 4 ounces ground turkey
- 2 green onions, chopped
- 2 slices of bacon, cooked, crumbled
- ¼ teaspoon dried thyme

Extra:
- ½ teaspoon salt
- ¼ teaspoon ground black pepper

Directions
1. Take a skillet pan, place it over medium heat, add bacon slices, and cook for 5 minutes until crispy.
2. Transfer bacon to a cutting board, cool for 5 minutes, then crumble it and set aside until required.
3. Add turkey into the pan, cook for 3 minutes until turkey is no longer pink, then add broccoli and onions, season with salt, black pepper, and thyme, stir well and continue cooking for 5 to 7 minutes until thoroughly cooked.
4. When done, top with bacon and serve.

Day 18
Breakfast – Celeriac Stuffed Avocado

Serving: 2
Preparation time: 10 minutes; Cooking time: 0 minutes
Nutritional Info: 285 Cal; 27 g Fats; 2.8 g Protein; 4.4 g Net Carb; 2.6 g Fiber;
Ingredients
- 1 avocado
- 1 celery root, finely chopped
- 2 tablespoons mayonnaise
- ½ of a lemon, juiced, zested
- 2 tablespoons mayonnaise

Extra:
- ¼ teaspoon salt

Directions
1. Prepare avocado and for this, cut avocado in half and then remove its pit.
2. Place remaining ingredients in a bowl, stir well until combined and evenly stuff this mixture into avocado halves.
3. Serve straight away.

Lunch – Bacon Wrapped Chicken Bites

Serving: 2
Preparation time: 10 minutes; Cooking time: 20 minutes
Nutritional Info: 153 Cal; 8.7 g Fats; 15 g Protein; 2.7 g Net Carb; 0.7 g Fiber;
Ingredients
- 1 chicken thigh, debone, cut into small pieces
- 4 slices of bacon, cut into thirds
- 2 tablespoons garlic powder

Extra:
- ¼ teaspoon salt
- 1/8 teaspoon ground black pepper

Directions
1. Switch on the oven, then set it to 400 degrees F and let it preheat.
2. Cut chicken into small pieces, then place them in a bowl, add salt, garlic powder, and black pepper and toss until well coated.
3. Wrap each chicken piece with a bacon strip, place in a baking dish and bake for 15 to 20 minutes until crispy, turning carefully every 5 minutes.
4. Serve straight away.

Dinner – Buttery Garlic Green Beans

Serving: 2
Preparation time: 5 minutes; Cooking time: 12 minutes
Nutritional Info: 224 Cal; 21.7 g Fats; 1.1 g Protein; 3.9 g Net Carb; 2.3 g Fiber;
Ingredients
- 6 ounces green beans
- 1 teaspoon minced garlic
- 1/8 teaspoon lemon pepper seasoning
- ½ cup of water
- 2 tablespoons mayonnaise

Extra:
- 2 tablespoons unsalted butter
- 1/3 teaspoon salt

Directions
1. Take a medium skillet pan, place it over medium heat, pour in water, and bring it to boil.
2. Switch heat to medium-low level, add green beans and cook for 5 minutes until beans start to soften.
3. Drain the beans, return them to the pan and place the pan over medium heat.
4. Add butter, stir, cook the beans for 3 minutes, then add garlic and continue cooking for 1 minute until fragrant.
5. Season green beans with lemon pepper and salt and cook for 3 minutes until beans have cooked and then serve straight away with mayonnaise.

Day 19
Breakfast – Fried Eggs

Serving: 2
Preparation time: 5 minutes; Cooking time: 8 minutes
Nutritional Info: 179 Cal; 16.5 g Fats; 7.6 g Protein; 0 g Net Carb; 0 g Fiber;
Ingredients
- 2 eggs
- 2 tablespoons unsalted butter

Extra:
- ¼ teaspoon salt
- 1/8 teaspoon ground black pepper

Directions
1. Take a skillet pan, place it over medium heat, add butter and when it has melted, crack eggs in the pan.
2. Cook eggs for 3 to 5 minutes until fried to the desired level, then transfer the eggs to serving plates and sprinkle with salt and black pepper.
3. Serve straight away.

Lunch – Broccoli, Green beans and Bacon Stir-fry

Serving: 2
Preparation time: 10 minutes; Cooking time: 13 minutes
Nutritional Info: 522 Cal; 47 g Fats; 22.2 g Protein; 0.5 g Net Carb; 2.1 g Fiber;
Ingredients
- 4 ounces broccoli florets
- 2 ounces green beans
- 4 slices of bacon, cooked, crumbled
- 1 tablespoon chopped parsley
- 1 tablespoon coconut oil

Extra:
- ½ teaspoon salt
- 1/8 teaspoon ground black pepper

Directions
1. Take a skillet pan, place it over medium heat, add bacon, and cook for 5 minutes until crispy.
2. Then transfer bacon to a cutting board, let it cool for 5 minutes, then crumble it and set aside until required.
3. Add broccoli and beans into the pan, add oil, season with salt and black pepper and cook for 5 to 7 minutes or until tender.
4. Return bacon into the pan, stir well, cook for 1 minute and then remove the pan from heat.
5. Garnish with parsley and serve.

Dinner – Slow Cooked Korean Pulled Chicken

Serving: 2
Preparation time: 5 minutes; Cooking time: 4 hours
Nutritional Info: 225 Cal; 12.3 g Fats; 27.6 g Protein; 1 g Net Carb; 0.2 g Fiber;

Ingredients
- 2 chicken thighs
- ½ teaspoon garlic powder
- 1 tablespoon stevia
- 2 tablespoons soy sauce
- ½ cup of water

Extra:
- 1 tablespoon coconut oil
- ¼ teaspoon salt

Directions
1. Grease the bottom and inner sides of a 4-quart slow cooker with a non-stick cooking spray.
2. Then season chicken on all sides with 1/2 teaspoon salt and place in a slow cooker.
3. Whisk together remaining ingredients until combined and then pour this mixture over chicken.
4. Cover and seal with its lid, then plugin and adjust the cooking timer for 4 hours and let cook at high heat setting.
5. When done, shred chicken with forks, then garnish with green onion and serve.

Day 20

Breakfast – Broccoli and Egg Muffin

Serving: 2
Preparation time: 10 minutes; Cooking time: 10 minutes
Nutritional Info: 76 Cal; 5.1 g Fats; 5.7 g Protein; 1.2 g Net Carb; 0.7 g Fiber;
Ingredients
- ¼ cup broccoli florets, steamed, chopped
- 2 tablespoons grated cheddar cheese
- 1/16 teaspoon dried thyme
- 1/16 teaspoon garlic powder
- 1 egg

Extra:
- ¼ teaspoon salt
- 1/8 teaspoon ground black pepper

Directions
1. Switch on the oven, then set it to 400 degrees F and let it preheat.
2. Meanwhile, take two silicone muffin cups, grease them with oil, and evenly fill them with broccoli and cheese.
3. Crack the egg in a bowl, add garlic powder, thyme, salt, and black pepper, whisk well, then evenly pour the mixture into muffin cups and bake for 8 to 10 minutes until done.
4. Serve straight away.

Lunch – Charred Green Beans with Pesto

Serving: 2
Preparation time: 5 minutes; Cooking time: 6 minutes

Nutritional Info: 265 Cal; 24.1 g Fats; 3.3 g Protein; 4.9 g Net Carb; 3.8 g Fiber;

Ingredients

- 6 ounces green beans
- 2 tablespoons coconut oil
- 3 tablespoons basil pesto
- ½ teaspoon stevia

Extra:

- 1/8 teaspoon salt
- 1/8 teaspoon ground black pepper

Directions

1. Place green beans in a heatproof bowl, cover with plastic wrap, poke holes in it with a fork, then microwave for 2 minutes and pat dry with paper towels.
2. Take a skillet pan, place it over medium-high heat, add oil and when it melts, add beans and cook for 4 to 5 minutes until slightly charred.
3. Remove pan from heat, add remaining ingredients, and stir well.
4. Serve straight away.

Dinner – Pesto Zucchini Noodles

Serving: 2
Preparation time: 5 minutes; Cooking time: 3 minutes
Nutritional Info: 384 Cal; 33 g Fats; 14.4 g Protein; 1.7 g Net Carb; 6 g Fiber;

Ingredients

- 2 zucchini, spiralized into noodles
- 2 tablespoons coconut oil
- 1/3 teaspoon salt
- 4 tablespoons pesto sauce
- 2 tablespoons chopped peanuts

Directions

1. Prepare zucchini noodles, and for this, cut zucchini into noodles by using a spiralizer or vegetable peeler.
2. Take a skillet pan, place it over medium heat, and add zucchini and cook for 3 minutes until it begins to soften.
3. Then add peanuts, season with salt, add pesto sauce and stir until well mixed.
4. Serve straight away.

Day 21
Breakfast – Chicken and Bacon Pancake

Serving: 2
Preparation time: 5 minutes; Cooking time: 8 minutes
Nutritional Info: 222 Cal; 17 g Fats; 16.5 g Protein; 0 g Net Carb; 0 g Fiber;
Ingredients
- 1 chicken thigh, debone
- 2 slices of bacon
- 1 egg
- 2 tablespoons coconut oil

Extra:
- ¼ teaspoon salt
- 1/8 teaspoon ground black pepper

Directions
1. Cut chicken into bite-size pieces, place them in a food processor, add bacon, egg, salt, and black pepper and process until well combined.
2. Take a frying pan, place it over medium heat, add 1 tablespoon oil and when hot, scoop chicken mixture in the pan, shape each scoop into a round pancake and cook for 4 minutes per side until brown and cooked.
3. When done, transfer pancakes into a plate, drizzle with remaining oil, and serve.

Lunch – Bacon Burger

Serving: 2
Preparation time: 5 minutes; Cooking time: 15 minutes
Nutritional Info: 262.5 Cal; 22.5 g Fats; 11 g Protein; 1.5 g Net Carb; 2 g Fiber;
Ingredients
- 2 ounces diced bacon

- 4 ounces ground turkey
- 2 tablespoons mustard paste

Extra:

- ¼ teaspoon salt
- ¼ teaspoon ground black pepper

Directions

1. Take a skillet pan, place it over medium heat, add bacon slices, and cook for 5 minutes until crispy.
2. Then transfer bacon to a cutting board, let it cool for 5 minutes, then chop them and transfer into a bowl.
3. Add remaining ingredients, except for mustard, stir well and shape the mixture into two patties.
4. Return pan over medium heat, add patties in it and then cook for 4 minutes per side.
5. Then smear patties with mustard and continue cooking for 1 minute until seared.
6. Serve straight away.

Dinner – Cinnamon Chicken Thighs

Serving: 2

Preparation time: 10 minutes; Cooking time: 20 minutes

Nutritional Info: 288 Cal; 22 g Fats; 18 g Protein; 1 g Net Carb; 0 g Fiber;

Ingredients

- 2 chicken thighs
- 1 teaspoon ground cinnamon
- 1 teaspoon chopped parsley
- 1/3 teaspoon dried basil
- 1/3 cup chicken broth

Extra:

- 1/3 teaspoon salt

Directions

1. Switch on the oven, then set it to 425 degrees F, and let it preheat.
2. Meanwhile, prepare spice mix and for this, place cinnamon, basil, salt, and parsley in a bowl and stir until mixed.
3. Take a casserole dish, pour in chicken broth from lemon chicken, add half of the spice mix and stir until mixed.

4. Coat chicken thighs with remaining spice mix, place them into the casserole dish and bake for 20 to 30 minutes until done, basting the chicken every 5 minutes with its sauce.
5. Serve straight away.

Week 4

Shopping List for Week 4

Remaining foods from the previous week(s):
- 6 ounces ground turkey
- Cilantro bunch
- 4 ounces Turkey bacon
- Peanuts

Look in pantry for:
- Himalayan pink salt/sea salt
- Organic black pepper
- Organic onion powder
- Organic garlic powder
- Organic minced garlic
- Organic Italian seasoning
- Organic dried basil
- Organic dried dill
- Organic dried
- Organic all-purpose seasoning
- Organic paprika
- Stevia
- Coconut oil
- Butter, unsalted
- Mayonnaise
- Apple Cider Vinegar

Purchase the following:

Items:	Store:	Quantity:	Price:
Large White Eggs, 12 Count	Walmart	1	1.07
Salmon Fillet 2 Lb.	Walmart	1	4
Salmon In Water	Walmart	1	1.7
Hass Avocados, Each	Walmart	1	1.1
Green Beans, 14.5 Oz.	Walmart	2	0.94
Cheddar Cheese Block 12 Oz.	Walmart	1	1.68
Cabbage Head, 3 Lb.	Walmart	1	1.74
Cut Asparagus	Walmart	1	1
Broccoli And Cauliflower Medley 12 Oz.	Walmart	1	1
Whipped Topping	Walmart	1	0.82
Lean Ground Beef 1 Lb.	Walmart	1	2.64
Chopped Spinach, 13.5 Oz.	Walmart	1	1.18
Green Bell Pepper	Walmart	1	0.53
Tomato Sauce 12 oz.	Walmart	1	0.5
		Total:	19.93

Day 22
Breakfast – Open Breakfast Sandwich

Serving: 2
Preparation time: 10 minutes; Cooking time: 13 minutes
Nutritional Info: 150.8 Cal; 13.5 g Fats; 5.5 g Protein; 1 g Net Carb; 0.8 g Fiber;
Ingredients
- 1 egg
- 2 ounces ground turkey
- 2 ounces ground beef
- 1 tablespoon whipped topping
- 2 ounces cheddar cheese, grated
- 1 teaspoon sriracha sauce

Extra:
- 1 teaspoon coconut oil
- ¾ teaspoon salt

- ½ teaspoon ground black pepper

Directions

- Place ground turkey and beef in a bowl, season with ½ teaspoon salt and ¼ teaspoon black pepper, stir until well mixed, and shape the mixture into two patties.
- Take a skillet pan, place it over medium heat, and when hot, add sausage patties and cook for 3 to 5 minutes per side until browned and thoroughly cooked, transfer patties to a plate and reserve the pan.
- Place grated cheese in a small heatproof bowl, add whipped topping, stir well, and microwave for 30 seconds until melted.
- Stir the cheese mixture, add sriracha sauce, stir well, and set aside until required.
- Crack the egg in a bowl, season with remaining salt and black pepper and whisk until combined.
- Return pan over medium-low heat, add oil and when hot, pour in the egg and cook for 3 minutes until omelet has cooked to the desired level.
- Assemble sandwich and for it, cut the omelet into half, then stuff with cheese mixture, place omelet on top of the patty and serve.

Lunch – Beef with Cabbage Noodles

Serving: 2
Preparation time: 5 minutes; Cooking time: 18 minutes
Nutritional Info: 188.5 Cal; 12.5 g Fats; 15.5 g Protein; 2.5 g Net Carb; 1 g Fiber;

Ingredients

- 4 ounces ground beef
- 1 cup chopped cabbage
- 4 ounces tomato sauce
- ½ teaspoon minced garlic
- ½ cup of water

Extra:

- ½ tablespoon coconut oil
- ½ teaspoon salt
- ¼ teaspoon Italian seasoning
- 1/8 teaspoon dried basil

Directions

1. Take a skillet pan, place it over medium heat, add oil and when hot, add beef and cook for 5 minutes until nicely browned.
2. Meanwhile, prepare the cabbage and for it, slice the cabbage into thin shred.
3. When the beef has cooked, add garlic, season with salt, basil, and Italian seasoning, stir well and continue cooking for 3 minutes until beef has thoroughly cooked.
4. Pour in tomato sauce and water, stir well and bring the mixture to boil.
5. Then reduce heat to medium-low level, add cabbage, stir well until well mixed and simmer for 3 to 5 minutes until cabbage is softened, covering the pan.
6. Uncover the pan and continue simmering the beef until most of the cooking liquid has evaporated.
7. Serve straight away.

Dinner – Garlic Butter Salmon

Serving: 2
Preparation time: 10 minutes; Cooking time: 15 minutes
Nutritional Info: 128 Cal; 4.5 g Fats; 41 g Protein; 1 g Net Carb; 0 g Fiber;
Ingredients
- 2 salmon fillets, skinless
- 1 teaspoon minced garlic
- 1 tablespoon chopped cilantro
- 1 tablespoon unsalted butter
- 2 tablespoons grated cheddar cheese

Extra:
- ½ teaspoon salt
- ¼ teaspoon ground black pepper

Directions
1. Switch on the oven, then set it to 350 degrees F, and let it preheat.
2. Meanwhile, taking a rimmed baking sheet, grease it with oil, place salmon fillets on it, season with salt and black pepper on both sides.
3. Stir together butter, cilantro, and cheese until combined, then coat the mixture on both sides of salmon in an even layer and bake for 15 minutes until thoroughly cooked.
4. Then switch on the broiler and continue baking the salmon for 2 minutes until the top is golden brown.
5. Serve straight away.

Day 23
Breakfast – Cabbage Hash Browns

Serving: 2
Preparation time: 10 minutes; Cooking time: 12 minutes
Nutritional Info: 336 Cal; 29.5 g Fats; 16 g Protein; 0.9 g Net Carb; 0.8 g Fiber;
Ingredients
- 1 ½ cup shredded cabbage
- 2 slices of bacon
- 1/2 teaspoon garlic powder
- 1 egg

Extra:
- 1 tablespoon coconut oil
- ½ teaspoon salt
- 1/8 teaspoon ground black pepper

Directions
1. Crack the egg in a bowl, add garlic powder, black pepper, and salt, whisk well, then add cabbage, toss until well mixed and shape the mixture into four patties.
2. Take a large skillet pan, place it over medium heat, add oil and when hot, add patties in it and cook for 3 minutes per side until golden brown.
3. Transfer hash browns to a plate, then add bacon into the pan and cook for 5 minutes until crispy.
4. Serve hash browns with bacon.

Lunch – Asparagus Sauté with Bacon

Serving: 2
Preparation time: 5 minutes; Cooking time: 10 minutes

Nutritional Info: 201 Cal; 16.1 g Fats; 9.5 g Protein; 1.7 g Net Carb; 2.8 g Fiber;

Ingredients

- 4 ounces chopped asparagus
- 2 slices of bacon, chopped

Extra:

- ½ teaspoon salt

Directions

1. Take a skillet pan, place it over medium heat, and when hot, add chopped bacon and cook for 3 minutes until sauté.
2. When done, transfer bacon to a plate, then add asparagus into the pan and cook for 5 minutes until tender.
3. Return bacon into the pan, season with salt, stir well and remove the pan from heat.
4. Serve straight away.

Dinner – Beef and Vegetable Skillet

Serving: 2

Preparation time: 5 minutes; Cooking time: 15 minutes

Nutritional Info: 332.5 Cal; 26 g Fats; 23.5 g Protein; 1.5 g Net Carb; 1 g Fiber;

Ingredients

- 3 ounces spinach, chopped
- ½ pound ground beef
- 2 slices of bacon, diced
- 2 ounces chopped asparagus

Extra:

- 3 tablespoons coconut oil
- 2 teaspoons dried thyme
- 2/3 teaspoon salt
- ½ teaspoon ground black pepper

Directions

1. Take a skillet pan, place it over medium heat, add oil and when hot, add beef and bacon and cook for 5 to 7 minutes until slightly browned.
2. Then add asparagus and spinach, sprinkle with thyme, stir well and cook for 7 to 10 minutes until thoroughly cooked.
3. Season skillet with salt and black pepper and serve.

Day 24
Breakfast – Egg and Cheese Breakfast

Serving: 2
Preparation time: 20 minutes; Cooking time: 5 minutes
Nutritional Info: 271 Cal; 21.5 g Fats; 17.6 g Protein; 1.1 g Net Carb; 0 g Fiber;
Ingredients
- 2 large eggs
- 2 blocks of cheddar cheese, each about 1-ounce

Directions
1. Take a medium saucepan, half full with water, add eggs in it, then place the pan over medium heat and bring to boil, covering with the lid.
2. When water starts boiling, remove the pan from heat and let it rest until eggs have cooked to the desired level, 4 minutes for the runny center, 6 minutes for the semi-soft center, 10 minutes for medium, and 16 minutes for hard-boiled.
3. Then drain the eggs, rinse it under cold water until cooled, and then peel them.
4. Serve eggs with cheese.

Lunch – Avocado and Salmon

Serving: 2
Preparation time: 10 minutes; Cooking time: 0 minutes
Nutritional Info: 525 Cal; 48 g Fats; 19 g Protein; 3 g Net Carb; 1 g Fiber;
Ingredients
- 1 avocado, halved, pitted
- 2 ounces flaked salmon, packed in water
- 1 tablespoon mayonnaise
- 1 tablespoon grated cheddar cheese

Extra:

- 1/8 teaspoon salt
- 2 tablespoons coconut oil

Directions
1. Prepare the avocado and for this, cut avocado in half and then remove its seed.
2. Drain the salmon, add it in a bowl along with remaining ingredients, stir well and then scoop into the hollow on an avocado half.
3. Serve straight away.

Dinner – Broccoli Cheese Casserole

Serving: 2
Preparation time: 10 minutes; Cooking time: 25 minutes
Nutritional Info: 163 Cal; 11 g Fats; 11.4 g Protein; 4 g Net Carb; 1 g Fiber;
Ingredients
- 6 ounces broccoli florets
- 2 eggs
- 1 tablespoon whipped topping
- 4 tablespoons grated cheddar cheese

Extra:
- ¼ teaspoon all-purpose seasoning
- 1/8 teaspoon ground black pepper

Directions
1. Switch on the oven, then set it to 375 degrees F, and let it preheat.
2. Meanwhile, cut broccoli into 1-inch pieces, then place them in a pot, pour in enough water to cover them and bring to boil over medium-high heat.
3. Switch heat to medium level, simmer broccoli for 4 to 5 minutes until tender-crisp and bright green and then drain them into a colander, set aside until cooled.
4. In the meantime, crack eggs in a bowl, add whipped topping, seasoning, and black pepper and beat until well combined.
5. Take a casserole dish, place cooled broccoli florets in it, sprinkle cheese on top, evenly pour in eggs, stir gently with a fork, and bake for 15 to 20 minutes until eggs have puffed up and the top is slightly browned.
6. Serve straight away.

Day 25
Breakfast – Cauliflower Hash Browns

Serving: 2
Preparation time: 10 minutes; Cooking time: 18 minutes
Nutritional Info: 347.8 Cal; 31 g Fats; 15.6 g Protein; 1.2 g Net Carb; 0.5 g Fiber;
Ingredients
- ¾ cup grated cauliflower
- 2 slices of bacon
- 1/2 teaspoon garlic powder
- 1 large egg white

Extra:
- 1 tablespoon coconut oil
- ½ teaspoon salt
- 1/8 teaspoon ground black pepper

Directions
1. Place grated cauliflower in a heatproof bowl, cover with plastic wrap, poke some holes in it with a fork and then microwave for 3 minutes until tender.
2. Let steamed cauliflower cool for 10 minutes, then wrap in a cheesecloth and squeeze well to drain moisture as much as possible.
3. Crack the egg in a bowl, add garlic powder, black pepper, and salt, whisk well, then add cauliflower, and toss until well mixed and sticky mixture comes together.
4. Take a large skillet pan, place it over medium heat, add oil and when hot, drop cauliflower mixture on it, press lightly to form hash brown patties, and cook for 3 to 4 minutes per side until browned.
5. Transfer hash browns to a plate, then add bacon into the pan and cook for 5 minutes until crispy.
6. Serve hash browns with bacon.

Lunch – Spinach Peanuts Stir-Fry

Serving: 2
Preparation time: 5 minutes; Cooking time: 5 minutes
Nutritional Info: 150 Cal; 11 g Fats; 7 g Protein; 4 g Net Carb; 2 g Fiber;
Ingredients
- 6 ounces spinach
- 3 tablespoons peanuts
- ¼ teaspoon salt
- 1 tablespoon coconut oil

Directions
1. Take a medium pot, place it over medium heat, add oil and when hot, add spinach and cook for 3 to 5 minutes until tender-crisp.
2. Then season with salt, remove the pot from heat, sprinkle with peanuts, and stir until mixed.
3. Serve straight away.

Dinner – Salmon with Green Beans

Serving: 2
Nutritional Info: 352 Cal; 29 g Fats; 19 g Protein; 3.5 g Net Carb; 1.5 g Fiber;
Ingredients
- 6 ounces green beans
- 3 ounces unsalted butter
- 2 salmon fillets

Extra:
- ½ teaspoon garlic powder
- ½ teaspoon salt
- ½ teaspoon cracked black pepper

Directions
1. Take a frying pan, place butter in it and when it starts to melts, add beans and salmon in fillets in it, season with garlic powder, salt, and black pepper, and cook for 8 minutes until salmon is cooked, turning halfway through and stirring the beans frequently.
2. When done, evenly divide salmon and green beans between two plates and serve.

Day 26
Breakfast – Asparagus, With Bacon and Eggs

Serving: 2
Preparation time: 5 minutes; Cooking time: 12 minutes
Nutritional Info: 179 Cal; 15.3 g Fats; 9 g Protein; 0.7 g Net Carb; 0.6 g Fiber;
Ingredients
- 4 ounces asparagus
- 2 slices of bacon, diced
- 1 egg

Extra:
- ¼ teaspoon salt
- 1/8 teaspoon ground black pepper

Directions
1. Take a skillet pan, place it over medium heat, add bacon, and cook for 4 minutes until crispy.
2. Transfer cooked bacon to a plate, then add asparagus into the pan and cook for 5 minutes until tender-crisp.
3. Crack the egg over the cooked asparagus, season with salt and black pepper, then switch heat to medium-low level and cook for 2 minutes until egg white has set.
4. Chop the cooked bacon slices, sprinkle over egg and asparagus and serve.

Lunch – Salmon Patties

Serving: 2
Preparation time: 5 minutes; Cooking time: 6 minutes
Nutritional Info: 276 Cal; 15.6 g Fats; 33.1 g Protein; 0.6 g Net Carb; 0.1 g Fiber;

Ingredients
- 4 ounces flaked salmon, packed in water
- 1 egg
- 2 tablespoons mayonnaise
- 1/8 teaspoon garlic powder
- 1 tablespoon chopped cilantro

Extra:
- 1 teaspoon coconut oil
- 1/8 teaspoon salt
- 1/16 teaspoon ground black pepper

Directions
1. Prepare the patties and for this, place all the ingredients in a bowl, stir well, and then shape the mixture into two patties.
2. Take a skillet pan, place it over medium heat, add oil and when hot, add salmon patties and cook for 3 minutes per side until golden brown.
3. Serve straight away.

Dinner – Cream of Asparagus Soup

Serving: 2
Preparation time: 10 minutes; Cooking time: 17 minutes
Nutritional Info: 124 Cal; 12.1 g Fats; 4.1 g Protein; 5 g Net Carb; 1.8 g Fiber;
Ingredients
- 0.5-ounce spinach
- 4 ounces chopped asparagus
- ½ teaspoon garlic powder
- 4 ounces whipped topping
- 1 ½ cup water

Extra:
- ½ tablespoon coconut oil
- ½ teaspoon salt
- ¼ teaspoon ground black pepper

Directions
1. Place a medium saucepan over medium heat, add oil and when hot, add asparagus, season with salt and black pepper and cook for 4 minutes until bright green.
2. Add garlic, stir well, cook for 1 minute until fragrant, then add water, stir well and bring the mixture to boil.

3. Switch heat to medium-low level, simmer for 10 minutes until asparagus is tender, then add spinach and continue cooking for 2 minutes.
4. Remove the pan from heat, puree the soup using an immersion blender and stir in whipped topping until combined.
5. Serve straight away.

Day 27
Breakfast – Meat and Eggs

Serving: 2
Preparation time: 10 minutes; Cooking time: 8 minutes
Nutritional Info: 325.5 Cal; 26.4 g Fats; 21.2 g Protein; 0.8 g Net Carb; 0 g Fiber;
Ingredients
- 4 ounces ground turkey
- 2 tablespoons unsalted butter
- 1 egg, beaten

Extra:
- ½ teaspoon salt
- 1/4 teaspoon ground black pepper

Directions
1. Take a skillet pan, place it over medium heat, add butter and when it melts, pour in eggs, season with 1/8 teaspoon salt, and 1/8 teaspoon black pepper and cook eggs for 3 minutes until scrambled to desire level.
2. Add ground turkey into the pan, season with remaining salt and black pepper and cook for 5 minutes until cooked.
3. Serve straight away.

Lunch – Coleslaw with Dill

Serving: 2
Preparation time: 35 minutes; Cooking time: 0 minutes
Nutritional Info: 137 Cal; 13 g Fats; 1 g Protein; 2 g Net Carb; 2 g Fiber;
Ingredients
- 1 ½ cups chopped cabbage
- 4 tablespoons mayonnaise
- ½ tablespoon apple cider vinegar
- ½ tablespoon dried dill

Extra:
- ½ teaspoon salt
- ¼ teaspoon stevia

Directions
1. Place mayonnaise in a bowl, add salt, dill, stevia, and vinegar and whisk until combined.
2. Add chopped cabbage, toss until well coated, and cool in the refrigerator for 30 minutes.
3. Serve straight away.

Dinner – Salmon Sheet pan

Serving: 2
Preparation time: 10 minutes; Cooking time: 20 minutes
Nutritional Info: 450 Cal; 23.8 g Fats; 36.9 g Protein; 5.9 g Net Carb; 2.4 g Fiber;
Ingredients
- 2 salmon fillets
- 2 ounces cauliflower florets
- 2 ounces broccoli florets
- 1 teaspoon minced garlic
- 1 tablespoon chopped cilantro

Extra:
- 2 tablespoons coconut oil
- 2/3 teaspoon salt
- ¼ teaspoon ground black pepper

Directions
1. Switch on the oven, then set it to 400 degrees F, and let it preheat.
2. Place oil in a small bowl, add garlic and cilantro, stir well, and microwave for 1 minute or until the oil has melted.

3. Take a rimmed baking sheet, place cauliflower and broccoli florets in it, drizzle with 1 tablespoon of coconut oil mixture, season with 1/3 teaspoon salt, 1/8 teaspoon black pepper and bake for 10 minutes.
4. Then push the vegetables to a side, place salmon fillets in the pan, drizzle with remaining coconut oil mixture, season with remaining salt and black pepper on both sides and bake for 10 minutes until salmon is fork-tender.
5. Serve straight away.

Day 28
Breakfast – Bell Pepper Eggs

Serving: 2
Preparation time: 10 minutes; Cooking time: 4 minutes
Nutritional Info: 110.5 Cal; 8 g Fats; 7.2 g Protein; 1.7 g Net Carb; 1.1 g Fiber;
Ingredients
- 1 green bell pepper,
- 2 eggs

Extra:
- 1 teaspoon coconut oil
- ¼ teaspoon salt
- ¼ teaspoon ground black pepper

Directions
1. Prepare pepper rings, and for this, cut out two slices from the pepper, about ¼-inch, and reserve remaining bell pepper for later use.
2. Take a skillet pan, place it over medium heat, grease it with oil, place pepper rings in it, and then crack an egg into each ring.
3. Season eggs with salt and black pepper, cook for 4 minutes or until eggs have cooked to the desired level.
4. Transfer eggs to a plate and serve.

Lunch – Bacon and Salmon Bites

Serving: 2
Preparation time: 10 minutes; Cooking time: 15 minutes
Nutritional Info: 120 Cal; 9 g Fats; 10 g Protein; 1 g Net Carb; 0.2 g Fiber;
Ingredients
- 1 salmon fillets
- 4 bacon slices, halved
- 2 tablespoons chopped cilantro

Extra:
- ¼ teaspoon salt
- 1/8 teaspoon ground black pepper

Directions
1. Switch on the oven, then set it to 350 degrees F, and let it preheat.
2. Meanwhile, cut salmon into bite-size pieces, then wrap each piece with a half slice of bacon, secure with a toothpick and season with salt and black pepper.
3. Take a baking sheet, place prepared salmon pieces on it and bake for 13 to 15 minutes until nicely browned and thoroughly cooked.
4. When done, sprinkle cilantro over salmon and serve.

Dinner – Beef, Pepper and Green Beans Stir-fry

Serving: 2
Preparation time: 5 minutes; Cooking time: 18 minutes
Nutritional Info: 282.5 Cal; 17.6 g Fats; 26.1 g Protein; 2.9 g Net Carb; 2.1 g Fiber;
Ingredients
- 6 ounces ground beef

- 2 ounces chopped green bell pepper
- 4 ounces green beans
- 3 tablespoons grated cheddar cheese

Extra:
- ½ teaspoon salt
- ¼ teaspoon ground black pepper
- ¼ teaspoon paprika

Directions
1. Take a skillet pan, place it over medium heat, add ground beef and cook for 4 minutes until slightly browned.
2. Then add bell pepper and green beans, season with salt, paprika, and black pepper, stir well and continue cooking for 7 to 10 minutes until beef and vegetables have cooked through.
3. Sprinkle cheddar cheese on top, then transfer pan under the broiler and cook for 2 minutes until cheese has melted and the top is golden brown.
4. Serve straight away.

 Week 5

Shopping List for Week 5

Remaining foods from the previous week(s):
- Tomato sauce
- Green beans 16.5 oz.
- 12-ounce cabbage
- Cilantro bunch

Look in pantry for:
- Himalayan pink salt/sea salt
- Organic black pepper
- Organic garlic powder
- Organic ginger powder
- Organic dried basil
- Organic dried thyme
- Organic dried oregano
- Organic paprika
- Organic all-purpose seasoning
- Organic cayenne pepper
- Organic red chili flakes
- Organic red chili powder
- Organic ground cumin
- Almonds
- Coconut oil
- Unsalted butter
- Mayonnaise

Purchase the following:

Items:	Store:	Quantity:	Price:
Large White Eggs, 12 Count	Walmart	1	1.07
Turkey Bacon, 12 oz.	Walmart	1	2.28
Ground Turkey Italian Roll, Frozen 1.0 lb.	Walmart	1	1.66
Avocad0	Walmart	1	0.56
Shredded Parmesan Cheese, 12 oz.	Walmart	1	1.46
Large Turnip, 3 Count	Walmart		1.38
Green Onion, bunch	Walmart	1	0.31
Chopped Spinach, 12 oz	Walmart	1	0.98
Jalapeno peppers, 5 Count	Walmart	1	0.2
Large Eggplant, 1 lb., 2 Count	Walmart	1	0.81
Zucchini	Walmart	2	1.3
Boneless Chicken Thighs, 10 Count	Walmart	1	5.2
Broccoli and Cauliflower, 12 oz.	Walmart	1	1
Lemon	Walmart	1	0.45
Large green bell pepper	Walmart	1	0.53
Cream cheese, 8 oz.	Walmart	1	0.76
		Total:	19.95

Day 29

Breakfast – Breakfast Cups

Serving: 2
Preparation time: 10 minutes; Cooking time: 15 minutes
Nutritional Info: 241 Cal; 16.3 g Fats; 22.3 g Protein; 0.7 g Net Carb; 1.2 g Fiber;
Ingredients
- 4 ounces ground turkey
- 2 tablespoons chopped spinach
- ¼ teaspoon garlic powder
- 2 eggs
- 1 tablespoon grated parmesan cheese

Extra:
- ½ teaspoon salt
- 1/3 teaspoon ground black pepper
- ½ teaspoon dried thyme
- 1/8 teaspoon paprika

Directions
- Switch on the oven, then set it to 400 degrees F, and let preheat.
- Meanwhile, place ground turkey in a bowl, season with 1/3 teaspoon salt, ¼ teaspoon black pepper, garlic, thyme and paprika, and stir well until combined.
- Take two silicone muffin cups, divide the turkey mixture between the cups, and then spread it evenly in the bottom and sides of the cup to create a muffin tin.
- Add 1 tablespoon chopped spinach and ½ tablespoon parmesan cheese into each cup, then crack an egg on top, season with remaining salt and black pepper, and bake for 15 to 20 minutes until meat is thoroughly cooked and eggs has cooked to the desired level.
- Serve straight away.

Lunch – Zucchini Noodles with Garlic and Parmesan

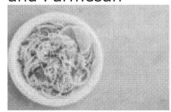

Serving: 2

Preparation time: 10 minutes; Cooking time: 6 minutes
Nutritional Info: 150 Cal; 16 g Fats; 1 g Protein; 0.5 g Net Carb; 1 g Fiber;
Ingredients
- 1 large zucchini, spiralized into noodles
- 2 tablespoons unsalted butter
- 1 ½ teaspoon minced garlic
- 2 tablespoons grated parmesan cheese

Extra:
- 1/3 teaspoon salt
- ¼ teaspoon red chili flakes
- ¼ teaspoon ground black pepper

Directions
1. Prepare zucchini noodles, and for this, cut zucchini into noodles by using a spiralizer or a vegetable peeler, and then set aside until required.
2. Take a skillet pan, place it over medium-high heat, add butter and garlic, cook for 1 minute until garlic is fragrant, then add zucchini noodles and continue cooking for 3 to 5 minutes until al dente.
3. When done, remove the

skillet pan from heat, season zucchini noodles with salt, red chili flakes, and black pepper, add cheese, and stir well until mixed.
4. Serve straight away.

Dinner – Chicken with Cauliflower

Serving: 2
Preparation time: 5 minutes; Cooking time: 20 minutes
Nutritional Info: 304 Cal; 25 g Fats; 16.3 g Protein; 1 g Net Carb; 1.25 g Fiber;
Ingredients
- 2 chicken thighs, boneless
- 6 ounces cauliflower florets
- 1 teaspoon ginger powder
- 2 tablespoons coconut oil
- ¼ cup mayonnaise

Extra:
- ¾ teaspoon salt
- ¼ teaspoon ground black pepper
- 1/8 teaspoon cayenne pepper

Directions
1. Switch on the oven, then set it to 400 degrees F, and let it preheat.
2. Meanwhile, brush chicken with oil and then season with ginger, ½ teaspoon salt, and cayenne pepper on both sides.
3. Place chicken on a baking dish and bake for 20 to 25 minutes until chicken is no longer pink and nicely golden.
4. While chicken is cooking, take a saucepan half full with salted water, place it over medium heat, bring it to boil, then add cauliflower florets and cook for 3 minutes or until slightly softened.
5. Drain cauliflower florets, transfer them to a bowl, add mayonnaise, season with remaining salt and black pepper, and stir until well mixed.
6. Serve chicken thighs with cauliflower.

Day 30

Breakfast – Bacon butter

Serving: 2
Preparation time: 5 minutes; Cooking time: 5 minutes
Nutritional Info: 150 Cal; 16 g Fats; 1 g Protein; 0.5 g Net Carb; 1 g Fiber;
Ingredients
- 2 ounces unsalted butter, softened
- 3 slices of bacon, chopped
- ½ teaspoon minced garlic
- ½ teaspoon dried basil
- ½ teaspoon tomato paste

For Extra:
- ¼ teaspoon salt
- ¼ teaspoon ground black pepper

Directions
1. Take a skillet pan, place it over medium heat, add 1 tablespoon butter and when it starts to melts, add chopped

bacon and cook for 5 minutes.
2. Then remove the pan from heat, add remaining butter, along with basil and tomato paste, season with salt and black pepper and stir until well mixed.
3. Transfer bacon butter into an airtight container, cover with the lid, and refrigerate for 1 hour until solid.
4. Serve straight away.

Lunch – Ground Turkey Chili

Serving: 2
Preparation time: 10 minutes; Cooking time: 27 minutes
Nutritional Info: 314 Cal; 20.1 g Fats; 24.1 g Protein; 6.8 g Net Carb; 4.1 g Fiber;
Ingredients
- 4 ounces ground turkey
- 1 jalapeno pepper, cored, cut into small cubes
- ½ teaspoon minced garlic
- 6 ounces tomato sauce
- ¾ cup of water

Extra:

- ½ tablespoon coconut oil
- ¾ teaspoon salt
- ¼ teaspoon red chili powder
- ½ teaspoon cumin
- ¼ teaspoon ground black pepper

Directions
1. Take a skillet pan, place it over medium heat, add oil and when it melts, add turkey and cook for 3 to 4 minutes until turkey is slightly brown.
2. Then add garlic and jalapeno pepper, season with salt, red chili powder, cumin, and black pepper, stir well, and continue cooking for 3 minutes.
3. Add tomato sauce, water, stir well and simmer the chili for 20 to 25 minutes until the sauce has reduced and thickened to the desired level.
4. Taste the chili to adjust seasoning and serve with sliced avocado.

Dinner – Garlic Chicken with Lemon

Serving: 2
Preparation time: 10 minutes; Cooking time: 20 minutes
Nutritional Info: 136 Cal; 9.7 g Fats; 10.5 g Protein; 0.8 g Net Carb; 0.3 g Fiber;
Ingredients
- 2 chicken thighs, boneless
- 1 tablespoon unsalted butter
- 2 teaspoons minced garlic
- 2 tablespoons chopped cilantro
- ½ of a lemon, juiced

Extra:

- 1 tablespoon melted coconut oil
- 1/3 teaspoon salt
- ¼ teaspoon ground black pepper

Directions
1. Switch on the oven, then set it to 450 degrees F, and let it preheat.
2. Meanwhile, take a baking pan, grease it with butter, place chicken thighs in it, season with salt and black pepper, and then drizzle with oil and lemon juice.

3. Sprinkle cilantro and garlic on top of chicken pieces and bake for 20

to 30 minutes until the chicken has cooked and

turned golden brown.
4. Serve straight away.

Day 31

Breakfast – Omelet-Stuffed Peppers

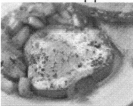

Serving: 2
Preparation time: 5 minutes; Cooking time: 20 minutes
Nutritional Info: 428 Cal; 35.2 g Fats; 23.5 g Protein; 2.8 g Net Carb; 1.5 g Fiber;
Ingredients
- 1 large green bell pepper, halved, cored
- 2 eggs
- 2 slices of bacon, chopped, cooked
- 2 tablespoons grated parmesan cheese

Extra:
- 1/3 teaspoon salt
- ¼ teaspoon ground black pepper

Directions
1. Switch on the oven, then set it to 400 degrees F, and let preheat.
2. Then take a baking dish, pour in 1 tablespoon water, place bell pepper halved in

it, cut-side up, and bake for 5 minutes.
3. Meanwhile, crack eggs in a bowl, add chopped bacon and cheese, season with salt and black pepper, and whisk until combined.
4. After 5 minutes of baking time, remove baking dish from the oven, evenly fill the peppers with egg mixture and continue baking for 15 to 20 minutes until eggs has set.
5. Serve straight away.

Lunch – Garlic and Parmesan Eggplant

Serving: 2
Preparation time: 10 minutes; Cooking time: 6 minutes
Nutritional Info: 136 Cal; 11 g Fats; 6 g

Protein; 2 g Net Carb; 3 g Fiber;
Ingredients
- 1/3 of a medium eggplant
- 1/3 of egg
- 2 tablespoons grated parmesan cheese
- ¾ teaspoon garlic powder

Extra:
- 2 tablespoons coconut oil
- ¼ teaspoon salt
- 1/8 teaspoon ground black pepper

Directions
1. Cut eggplant into 1/3 inch thick slices, then arrange them on a plate in a single layer, sprinkle with 1/8 teaspoon salt, let sit for 30 minutes and then pat dry the slices of eggplant with paper towels.
2. Crack the egg in a bowl and whisk until combined.
3. Place cheese in a shallow dish, add remaining salt, black pepper, and garlic powder and stir until mixed.

4. Working on one slice at a time, first coat the eggplant slices in egg and then dredge with parmesan cheese mixture until coated, coat the remaining eggplant slices in the same manner.

5. Take a skillet pan, place it over medium heat, add oil and when it melts, add coated eggplant slices and cook for 2 to 3 minutes per side until browned and crispy.

6. When done, remove eggplant slices from the pan and then transfer them to a plate lined with paper towels.

7. Serve straight away.

Dinner – Burgers with Tomato Butter

Serving: 2
Preparation time: 10 minutes; Cooking time: 13 minutes

Nutritional Info: 192.8 Cal; 16.7 g Fats; 8.5 g Protein; 2.5 g Net Carb; 1.25 g Fiber;

Ingredients

- 4 ounces ground turkey
- 4 ounces unsalted butter
- 4 ounce shredded cabbage
- ½ teaspoon tomato sauce

Extra:

- 1 ¼ teaspoon salt
- ¾ teaspoon ground black pepper
- ½ teaspoon thyme

Directions

1. Switch on the oven, then set it to 220 degrees F, and let it preheat.

2. Meanwhile, prepare patties and for this, place ground turkey in a bowl, add ½ teaspoon salt, ¼ teaspoon black pepper, thyme, stir well and then shape the mixture into two patties.

3. Take a frying pan, add 1-ounce butter in it, and when it melted, add chicken patties and cook for 3 to 4 minutes per side until nicely browned and cooked.

4. When done, transfer patties to a plate and set aside, then add 1-ounce butter in the pan and when it melts, add cabbage.

5. Switch heat to medium-high level, season with ½ teaspoon salt, ¼ teaspoon ground black pepper, and cook for 3 to 5 minutes until the cabbage has fried, and when done, transfer the cabbage to a plate.

6. Prepare tomato butter and for this, place remaining butter in a small bowl, add tomato sauce, add remaining salt and black pepper and stir well by using an electric mixer until mixed.

7. Serve patties with fried cabbage and tomato butter.

Day 32

Breakfast – Bacon Avocado Bombs

Serving: 2
Preparation time: 10 minutes; Cooking time: 10 minutes
Nutritional Info: 378 Cal; 33.6 g Fats; 15.1 g Protein; 0.5 g Net Carb; 2.3 g Fiber;
Ingredients
- 1 avocado, halved, pitted
- 4 slices of bacon
- 2 tablespoons grated parmesan cheese

Directions
1. Switch on the oven and broiler and let it preheat.
2. Meanwhile, prepare the avocado and for that, cut it in half, then remove its pit, and then peel the skin.
3. Evenly one half of the avocado with cheese, replace with the other half of avocado and then wrap avocado with bacon slices.
4. Take a baking sheet, line it with aluminum foil, place wrapped avocado on it, and broil for 5 minutes per side, flipping carefully with tong halfway.
5. When done, cut each avocado in half crosswise and serve

Lunch – Easy Cheesy Zoodles

Serving: 2
Preparation time: 5 minutes; Cooking time: 10 minutes
Nutritional Info: 107 Cal; 9 g Fats; 2 g Protein; 2 g Net Carb; 1 g Fiber;
Ingredients
- 1 large zucchini, spiralized into noodles
- 1/8 teaspoon garlic powder
- 2 tablespoons softened cream cheese
- 1 tablespoon grated parmesan cheese

Extra:
- ½ tablespoon coconut oil
- 1/3 teaspoon salt
- ¼ teaspoon ground black pepper

Directions
1. Prepare zucchini noodles, and for this, cut zucchini into noodles by using a spiralizer or a vegetable peeler.
2. Then take a skillet pan, place it over medium-high heat, add zucchini noodles and garlic, toss well until mixed, and cook for 4 minutes until slightly soft.
3. Push noodles to one side of the pan, add cream cheese into the other side of the pan, stir it until melts, then mix with noodles until coated and season with salt and black pepper.
4. Remove pan from heat, sprinkle zoodles with parmesan cheese and serve.

Dinner – Green Beans with Almonds

Serving: 2
Preparation time: 5 minutes; Cooking time: 6 minutes
Nutritional Info: 100 Cal; 100 g Fats; 100 g Protein; 100 g Net Carb; 100 g Fiber;
Ingredients
- 6 ounces green beans
- 1 tablespoon lemon juice

- 1 teaspoon minced garlic
- 3 tablespoons sliced almonds

Extra:
- ¼ teaspoon salt
- 1 tablespoon coconut oil

Directions
1. Place green beans in a heatproof bowl, cover it with plastic wrap, poke holes in it by using a fork and then microwave for 2 minutes until beans are tender-crisp.
2. Drain the beans, place them in another bowl, drizzle with lemon juice, season with salt and toss well until mixed.
3. Take a skillet pan, place it over medium heat, add oil and when hot, add sliced almonds and cook for 3 minutes until slightly browned.
4. Add garlic, stir well, cook for 1 minute until fragrant and light brown and then transfer the almond-garlic mixture into green beans bowl.
5. Toss well until mixed and serve.

Day 33

Breakfast –Egg in a Hole with Eggplant

Serving: 2
Preparation time: 5 minutes; Cooking time: 15 minutes
Nutritional Info: 184 Cal; 14.1 g Fats; 7.8 g Protein; 3 g Net Carb; 3.5 g Fiber;
Ingredients
- 1 large eggplant
- 2 eggs
- 1 tablespoon coconut oil, melted
- 1 teaspoon unsalted butter
- 2 tablespoons chopped green onions

Extra:
- ¾ teaspoon ground black pepper
- ¾ teaspoon salt

Directions
1. Set the grill and let it preheat at the high setting.
2. Meanwhile, prepare the eggplant, and for this, cut two slices from eggplant, about 1-inch thick, and reserve the remaining eggplant for later use.
3. Brush slices of eggplant with oil, season with salt on both sides, then place the slices on grill and cook for 3 to 4 minutes per side.
4. Transfer grilled eggplant to a cutting board, let it cool for 5 minutes and then make a home in the center of each slice by using a cookie cutter.
5. Take a frying pan, place it over medium heat, add butter and when it melts, add eggplant slices in it and crack an egg into its each hole.
6. Let the eggs cook for 3 to 4 minutes, then carefully flip the eggplant slice and continue cooking for 3 minutes until the egg has thoroughly cooked.

7. Season egg with salt and black pepper, transfer them to a plate, then garnish with green onions and serve.

Lunch – Keto Potatoes

Serving: 2
Preparation time: 5 minutes; Cooking time: 15 minutes
Nutritional Info: 88 Cal; 9 g Fats; 3 g Protein; 3.5 g Net Carb; 1 g Fiber;
Ingredients
- 1 large turnip, peeled, diced
- 1/4 of a spring onion, diced, and more for garnishing
- 2 slices of bacon, chopped
- 1 tablespoon olive oil
- 1 tablespoon softened cream cheese

Extra:
- 1/2 teaspoon paprika
- 1/2 teaspoon garlic powder
- 1/2 teaspoon salt
- 1/2 teaspoon ground black pepper

Directions
1. Take a skillet pan, place it over medium-high heat add oil and when hot, add diced turnip, season with salt, black pepper, and paprika, sprinkle with garlic, stir well and cook for 5 minutes.
2. Then add onion, stir and continue cooking for 3 minutes until onions start to soften.
3. Add chopped bacon, continue cooking for 5 to 7 minutes, or until bacon is crispy and remove the pan from heat.
4. Top with green onions and cream cheese and then serve straight away.

Dinner – Eggplant and Chicken Casserole

Serving: 2
Preparation time: 5 minutes; Cooking time: 30 minutes
Nutritional Info: 169 Cal; 9 g Fats; 18 g Protein; 2 g Net Carb; 2 g Fiber;
Ingredients
- 2 chicken thighs, boneless

- ¼ teaspoon garlic powder
- 1/3 of a large eggplant
- 2 tablespoons grated parmesan cheese
- 1 tablespoon tomato sauce

Extra:
- 1 ¼ teaspoon coconut oil
- 1/4 teaspoon salt
- 1/4 teaspoon ground black pepper
- ½ teaspoon dried oregano

Directions
1. Switch on the oven, then set it to 375 degrees F, and let it preheat.
2. Prepare chicken thighs and for this, butterfly each chicken thigh, then pound them by using a meat mallet, until 1/4-inch thick and then season one side of chicken with 1/8 teaspoon each of salt and black pepper on both side.
3. Take a skillet pan, place it over medium-high heat, add 2/3 teaspoon oil and when hot, add chicken in it, seasoned side down, and cook for 7 minutes per side until golden browned, set

aside until required.

4. While chicken cooks, take the reserved eggplant from previous recipes and cut it into two slices.
5. Place eggplant slices onto a baking sheet lined with

parchment paper, drizzle with ¼ teaspoon oil and season with ¼ teaspoon oregano, 1/8 teaspoon each of salt and black pepper on each slice.
6. When the chicken has cooked, top a piece of chicken

over each slice of eggplant, then top with tomato sauce and cheese and bake for 15 minutes until cheese starts bubbling and the top is golden brown.
7. Serve straight away.

Day 34

Breakfast – Frittata with Spinach and Meat

Serving: 2
Preparation time: 10 minutes; Cooking time: 20 minutes
Nutritional Info: 166 Cal; 13 g Fats; 10 g Protein; 0.5 g Net Carb; 0.5 g Fiber;
Ingredients
- 4 ounces ground turkey
- 3 ounces of spinach leaves
- 1/3 teaspoon minced garlic
- 1/3 teaspoon coconut oil
- 2 eggs
Extra:
- 1/3 teaspoon salt
- ¼ teaspoon ground black pepper
Directions

1. Switch on the oven, then set it to 400 degrees F, and let it preheat.
2. Meanwhile, take a skillet pan, place it over medium heat, add spinach and cook for 3 to 5 minutes until spinach leaves have wilted, remove the pan from heat.
3. Take a small heatproof skillet pan, place it over medium heat, add ground turkey and cook for 5 minutes until thoroughly cooked.
4. Then add spinach, season with salt and black pepper, stir well, then remove the pan from heat and

spread the mixture evenly in the pan.
5. Crack eggs in a bowl, season with salt and black pepper, then pour this mixture over spinach mixture in the pan and bake for 10 to 15 minutes until frittata has thoroughly cooked and the top is golden brown.
6. When done, let frittata rest in the pan for 5 minutes, then cut it into slices and serve.

Lunch – Garlic Spinach

Serving: 2

Preparation time: 5 minutes; Cooking time: 5 minutes
Nutritional Info: 155 Cal; 14 g Fats; 4 g Protein; 2 g Net Carb; 6 g Fiber;
Ingredients
- 1 tablespoon coconut oil
- 8 ounces of spinach leaves
- 1 ½ teaspoon minced garlic

Extra:
- ¼ teaspoon salt

Directions
1. Take a frying pan, place it over medium heat, add oil and when hot, add spinach and cook for 5 minutes until its leaves wilts.
2. Then add garlic and salt, stir well and continue cooking for 2 minutes.
3. Serve straight away.

Dinner – Chicken Salad

Serving: 2
Preparation time: 10 minutes; Cooking time: 12 minutes
Nutritional Info: 192 Cal; 15 g Fats; 12 g Protein; 0.5 g Net Carb; 1.5 g Fiber;
Ingredients
- 2 chicken thighs, boneless
- 1 ½ cup water
- 2 tablespoons mayonnaise
- 1 green onion, sliced
- 2 tablespoons chopped cilantro

Extra:
- 1 tablespoon coconut oil
- ½ teaspoon salt

Directions
1. Switch on the instant pot, press the sauté button, add oil and let heat until it melts.
2. Season chicken with salt, add it into the instant pot, and cook for 4 minutes per side.
3. Pour in water, shut with lid, and cook on manual setting for 3 minutes at high pressure.
4. When done, do natural pressure release, then transfer chicken to a cutting board and shred it by using two forks, reserve chicken broth for later use.
5. Prepare salad and for this, transfer chicken to a bowl, add remaining ingredients and toss until combined.
6. Taste the salad to adjust seasoning and serve straight away.

Day 35

Breakfast – Jalapeno and Cheese Egg Muffins

Serving: 2

Preparation time: 10 minutes; Cooking time: 15 minutes
Nutritional Info: 108 Cal; 7.1 g Fats; 8.9 g Protein; 1.8 g Net Carb; 0.4 g Fiber;
Ingredients

- 1 jalapeno pepper, diced
- 2 tablespoons sliced green onions
- 2 tablespoons grated parmesan cheese

- 1 teaspoon all-purpose seasoning
- 2 eggs

Extra:

- 1/3 teaspoon salt
- ¼ teaspoon ground black pepper

Directions

1. Switch on the oven, then set it to 375 degrees F, and let it preheat.
2. Meanwhile, take two silicone muffin cups, grease with oil, and evenly fill them with cheese, jalapeno pepper, and green onion.
3. Crack eggs in a bowl, season with salt, black pepper, and all-purpose seasoning, whisk well, then evenly pour the mixture into muffin cups and bake for 15 to 20 minutes or until the top is slightly brown and muffins have puffed up.
4. Serve straight away.

Lunch – Taco Turnip Wedges

Serving: 2

Preparation time: 5 minutes; Cooking time: 20 minutes
Nutritional Info: 129 Cal; 12.6 g Fats; 1.7 g Protein; 4.3 g Net Carb; 2.2 g Fiber;
Ingredients

- 2 large turnips
- ¾ teaspoon onion powder
- ½ teaspoon garlic powder
- 1 ½ tablespoon melted coconut oil
- 1 tablespoon cream cheese

Extra:

- ½ teaspoon salt
- 1 tablespoon red chili powder
- 2/3 tablespoon cumin
- ¼ teaspoon dried oregano

Directions

1. Switch on the oven, then set it to 350 degrees F, and let it preheat.
2. Prepare taco seasoning and for this, stir together salt, onion powder, garlic powder, red chili powder, cumin, and oregano and set aside until required.
3. Peel the turnips, cut into wedges, then place them in a plastic bag, add prepared taco seasoning, then add oil, seal the bag and turn it upside down until well coated.
4. Transfer the mixture onto a baking sheet, spread the wedges evenly, and bake for 20 minutes until golden brown and cooked.
5. Top with cream cheese and serve straight away.

Dinner – Broccoli Fritters

Serving: 2
Preparation time: 10 minutes; Cooking time: 10 minutes
Nutritional Info: 170.5 Cal; 14 g Fats; 6.8 g Protein; 3.1 g Net Carb; 2 g Fiber;
Ingredients

- 6 ounces broccoli florets, chopped
- 1 teaspoon garlic powder
- 1 egg
- 1 tablespoon grated parmesan cheese
- 2 tablespoons mayonnaise

Extra:

- 1 teaspoon onion powder
- 2/3 teaspoon salt
- ¼ teaspoon ground black pepper

Directions

1. Switch on the oven, then set it to 400 degrees F, and let it preheat.

2. Place chopped broccoli florets in a bowl, add them in a food processor and pulse for 1 minute until finely chopped.

3. Tip broccoli in a bowl, add remaining ingredients, and stir until well combined.

4. Take a baking sheet, grease it with oil, then drop scoops of prepared broccoli mixture, shape it into patties and bake for 7 to 10 minutes until golden brown.

5. Serve fritters with mayonnaise.

Shopping List for Week 2

Remaining foods from the previous week(s):
- 3 ounces tomato sauce with basil, garlic, and oregano
- 2 ounces whipped topping
- 8 ounces ground turkey
- 4 ounces Tri-color Cole Slaw
- 4 ½ avocados
- 3 ounces of turkey bacon
- 2 ounces cheddar cheese

Look in pantry for:
- Minced garlic
- Himalayan pink salt/sea salt
- Organic black pepper
- Organic paprika
- Organic cinnamon
- Organic ground cardamom
- Hot paprika
- Smoked paprika
- Red pepper flakes
- Seafood seasoning
- Taco seasoning
- Swerve sweetener
- Liquid stevia
- Psyllium husk
- Fennel seeds
- Sesame seeds
- Butter, unsalted
- Olive oil
- Avocado oil
- Soy sauce, low-sodium
- Apple cider vinegar
- Mayonnaise
- Sweet chili sauce

Purchase the following:

Items:	Store:	Quantity:	Price:
Large white eggs, 6 count, 12 ounce	Walmart	3	1.78
Jalapeno pepper, 4 - 5 count	Walmart	1	0.18
Cream cheese, 12 oz.	Walmart	1	0.8
Turkey bacon, 12 oz.	Walmart	1	2.21
Salmon fillets, skinless, 2 lb., 8 count	Walmart	1	4
Boneless skinless chicken thighs, 2.5 lb. 8 count	Walmart	1	5.21
Red bell peppers, 3 count	Walmart	1	1.04
Broccoli and cauliflower florets 12 oz.	Walmart	1	1
Iceberg lettuce, chopped, 12 oz.	Walmart	1	0.68
Tuna, packed in water, 6 oz.	Walmart	1	0.81
Fresh spinach, 10 oz.	Walmart	1	1.23
Lime, count 1	Walmart	1	0.16
Chives, 0.25 oz.	Walmart	1	0.88
		Total:	19.98

Day 43

Breakfast – Buttery Scrambled Eggs

Serving: 2
Preparation time: 5 minutes; Cooking time: 6 minutes
Nutritional Info: 81.5 Cal; 3.75 g Fats; 3.75 g Protein; 0.25 g Net Carb; 0 g Fiber;
Ingredients
- 3 eggs
- ¼ teaspoon salt
- 1/8 teaspoon ground black pepper
- 2 tablespoons chopped unsalted butter, cold
- 1 tablespoon unsalted butter, softened

Directions
- Take a bowl, cracked eggs in it, whisk until well combined, and then stir in chopped cold butter until mixed.
- Take a skillet pan, place it over medium-low heat, add butter and when it melts, pour in the egg mixture and cook for 1 minute, don't stir.
- Then stir the omelet and cook for 1 to 2 minutes until thoroughly cooked and scramble to the desired level.
- Season scramble eggs with salt and black pepper and then serve.

Lunch – Jalapeño Poppers

Serving: 2
Preparation time: 5 minutes; Cooking time: 10 minutes
Nutritional Info: 78.5 Cal; 4 g Fats; 1.5 g Protein; 1.3 g Net Carb; 0.2 g Fiber;
Ingredients
- 4 jalapeno peppers
- 8 strips of bacon
- 4 ounces cream cheese

Extra:
- ¼ teaspoon salt
- 1/8 teaspoon ground black pepper

Directions
- Switch on the oven, then set it to 400 degrees F and let it preheat.
- Meanwhile, cut each pepper in half lengthwise, remove and discard the seeds and then fill the peppers with cream cheese.
- Wrap each pepper with bacon and cook for 10 minutes until peppers are tender and bacon is nicely golden brown.
- Serve straight away.

Dinner – Bacon wrapped Salmon

Serving: 2
Preparation time: 5 minutes; Cooking time: 10 minutes
Nutritional Info: 190.7 Cal; 16.5 g Fats; 10.5 g Protein; 0 g Net Carb; 0 g Fiber;
Ingredients
- 2 salmon fillets, cut into four pieces
- 4 slices of bacon
- 2 teaspoons olive oil
- 2 tablespoons mayonnaise

Extra:
- ½ teaspoon salt
- ½ teaspoon ground black pepper

Directions
- Switch on the oven, then set it to 375 degrees F and let it preheat.
- Meanwhile, place a skillet pan, place it over medium-high

heat, add oil and let it heat.

- Season salmon fillets with salt and black pepper, wrap each salmon fillet with a bacon

slice, then add to the pan and cook for 4 minutes, turning halfway through.

- Then transfer skillet pan containing

salmon into the oven and cook salmon for 5 minutes until thoroughly cooked.

- Serve salmon with mayonnaise

Day 44
Breakfast – Cream Cheese Pancakes

Serving: 2
Preparation time: 5 minutes; Cooking time: 5 minutes
Nutritional Info: 97.8 Cal; 8.4 g Fats; 4.4 g Protein; 1 g Net Carb; 0.2 g Fiber;
Ingredients
- 2 ounces cream cheese
- 2 eggs
- ½ teaspoon cinnamon
- 1 teaspoon unsalted butter

Directions
- Place cream cheese in a blender, add eggs and cinnamon, pulse for 1 minute or until smooth, and then let the batter rest for 5 minutes.
- Take a skillet pan, place it over medium heat, add butter and

when it melts, drop one-fourth of the batter into the pan, spread evenly, and cook the pancakes for 2 minutes per side until done.

- Transfer pancakes to a plate and serve.

Lunch – Paprika Rubbed Chicken

Serving: 2
Preparation time: 5 minutes; Cooking time: 25 minutes
Nutritional Info: 102.3 Cal; 8 g Fats; 7.2 g Protein; 0.3 g Net Carb; 0.3 g Fiber;
Ingredients
- 2 chicken thighs, boneless
- ¼ tablespoon fennel seeds, ground
- ½ teaspoon hot paprika
- ¼ teaspoon smoked paprika
- ½ teaspoon minced garlic

Extra:
- ¼ teaspoon salt
- 2 tablespoons olive oil

Directions
- Switch on the oven, then set it to 325 degrees F and let it preheat.
- Prepare the spice mix and for this, take a small bowl, add all the ingredients in it, except for chicken, and stir until well mixed.
- Brush the mixture on all sides of the chicken, rub it well into the meat, then place chicken onto a baking sheet and roast for 15 to 25 minutes until thoroughly cooked, basting every 10 minutes with the drippings.
- Serve straight away.

Dinner – Cheesy Chicken Stuffed Bell Pepper

Serving: 2
Preparation time: 5 minutes; Cooking time: 18 minutes
Nutritional Info: 114.3 Cal; 8.3 g Fats; 7 g Protein; 2.5 g Net Carb; 1 g Fiber;
Ingredients
- 4 ounces ground turkey
- 2 medium red bell peppers, cored, destemmed
- 2 ounces cream cheese, softened
- 2 ounces grated cheddar cheese
- 2 tablespoons tomato sauce

Extra:
- ¼ teaspoon salt
- 1/3 teaspoon paprika
- 1/8 teaspoon ground black pepper

Directions
- Switch on the oven, then set it to 350 degrees F and let it preheat.
- Then prepare bell peppers, place them on a baking sheet lined with parchment sheet, spray with olive oil and bake for 6 minutes.
- Meanwhile, take a skillet pan and when hot, add turkey, season with salt, paprika, and black pepper and cook for 7 minutes until golden brown.
- When done, distribute half of the turkey between bell peppers, then top with 1 tablespoon cream cheese and tomato sauce, and cover with remaining turkey.
- Top turkey evenly with cheddar cheese and broil for 3 minutes until cheese has melted and golden brown.
- Serve straight away.

Day 45

Breakfast – Bacon and Avocado Salad

Serving: 2
Preparation time: 5 minutes; Cooking time: 8 minutes
Nutritional Info: 147.6 Cal; 13.6 g Fats; 6 g Protein; 1.7 g Net Carb; 0.6 g Fiber;
Ingredients
1. 4 slices of bacon, chopped
2. 4 ounces chopped lettuce
3. ½ of a medium avocado, sliced
4. 1 tablespoon olive oil
5. 1 tablespoon apple cider vinegar

Directions
- Prepare bacon and for this, place a skillet pan over medium heat and when hot, add chopped bacon and cook for 5 to 8 minutes until golden brown.
- Then distribute lettuce and avocado between two plates, top with bacon, drizzle with olive oil and apple cider and serve.

Lunch – Turkey and Broccoli Bowl

Serving: 2

Preparation time: 5 minutes; Cooking time: 15 minutes
Nutritional Info: 120.3 Cal; 8.3 g Fats; 8.4 g Protein; 2 g Net Carb; 1 g Fiber;
Ingredients
1. 4 ounces ground turkey
2. 4 ounces broccoli florets
3. 4 ounces cauliflower florets, riced
4. 1 teaspoon soy sauce
5. ¼ teaspoon red pepper flakes

Extra:
6. 1/3 teaspoon salt
7. ¼ teaspoon ground black pepper
8. 1 tablespoon olive oil

Directions
- Take a skillet pan, place it over medium heat, add olive oil and when hot, add beef, crumble it and cook for 8 minutes until no longer pink.
- Then add broccoli florets and riced cauliflower, stir well, drizzle with soy sauce and sesame oil, season with salt, black pepper, and red pepper flakes and

continue cooking for 5 minutes until vegetables have thoroughly cooked.
- Serve straight away.

Dinner – Stir fry Tuna with Vegetables

Serving: 2
Preparation time: 5 minutes; Cooking time: 15 minutes
Nutritional Info: 99.7 Cal; 5.1 g Fats; 11 g Protein; 1.6 g Net Carb; 1 g Fiber;
Ingredients
- 4 ounces tuna, packed in water
- 2 ounces broccoli florets
- ½ of red bell pepper, cored, sliced
- ½ teaspoon minced garlic
- ½ teaspoon sesame seeds

Extra:
- 1 tablespoon olive oil
- 2/3 teaspoon soy sauce
- 2/3 teaspoon apple cider vinegar

- 3 tablespoons water

Directions
- Take a skillet pan, add ½ tablespoon oil and when hot, add bell pepper and cook for 3 minutes until tender-crisp.
- Then add broccoli floret, drizzle with water and continue cooking for 3 minutes until steamed, covering the pan.
- Uncover the pan, cook for 2 minutes until all the liquid has evaporated, and then push bell pepper to one side of the pan.
- Add remaining oil to the other side of the pan, add tuna and cook for 3 minutes until seared on all sides.
- Then drizzle with soy sauce and vinegar, toss all the ingredients in the pan until mixed and sprinkle with sesame seeds.
- Serve straight away.

Day 46

Breakfast – Spinach and Eggs Scramble

Serving: 2
Preparation time: 5 minutes; Cooking time: 10 minutes
Nutritional Info: 90 Cal; 7 g Fats; 5.6 g Protein; 0.7 g Net Carb; 0.6 g Fiber;
Ingredients
- 4 ounces spinach
- ¼ teaspoon salt
- 1/8 teaspoon ground black pepper
- 1 tablespoon unsalted butter
- 3 eggs, beaten

Directions
- Take a frying pan, place it over medium heat, add butter and when it melts, add spinach and cook for 5 minutes until leaves have wilted.
- Then pour in eggs, season with salt and black pepper, and cook for 3 minutes until eggs have scramble to the desired level.
- Serve straight away.

Lunch – Panini Styled Mayo Salmon

Serving: 2
Preparation time: 5 minutes; Cooking time: 10 minutes
Nutritional Info: 132.7 Cal; 11.1 g Fats; 8 g Protein; 0.3 g Net Carb; 0 g Fiber;
Ingredients
- 2 salmon fillets
- 4 tablespoons mayonnaise

Directions
- Switch on the Panini press, spray it with oil and let it preheat.
- Then spread 1 tablespoon of mayonnaise on each side of salmon, place them on Panini press pan, shut with lid, and cook for 7 to 10 minutes until salmon has cooked to the desired level.
- Serve straight away.

Dinner – Grilled Spiced Chicken Thighs

Serving: 2
Preparation time: 5 minutes; Cooking time: 10 minutes
Nutritional Info: 97.2 Cal; 8.2 g Fats; 5.8 g Protein; 0.2 g Net Carb; 0 g Fiber;
Ingredients
- 2 chicken thighs, boneless
- 1 teaspoon seafood seasoning
- 2 tablespoons unsalted butter, melted
- 1 tablespoon olive oil

Directions
- Take a shallow dish, place chicken thighs in it, add oil and ½ teaspoon seasoning and toss until well coated.
- Then take a grill pan, place it over medium heat, spray it with oil and when hot, add chicken thighs and cook for 10 minutes until cooked.
- Meanwhile, place butter in a separate dish bowl, add remaining

seasoning, and stir until combined.

Day 47
Breakfast – Sheet Pan Eggs

Serving: 2
Preparation time: 5 minutes; Cooking time: 8 minutes
Nutritional Info: 87 Cal; 5.4 g Fats; 7.2 g Protein; 1.7 g Net Carb; 0.7 g Fiber;
Ingredients
- ½ of medium red bell pepper, chopped
- 2 tablespoons chopped chives
- 2 eggs

Extra:
- ¼ teaspoon salt
- 1/8 teaspoon ground black pepper

Directions
- Switch on the oven, then set it to 350 degrees F and let it preheat.
- Meanwhile, crack eggs in a bowl, add remaining ingredients and whisk until combined.
- Take a small heatproof dish, pour in egg mixture, and

bake for 5 to 8 minutes until set.
- When done, cut it into two squares and then serve.

Lunch – Lettuce and Avocado Salad

Serving: 2
Preparation time: 5 minutes; Cooking time: 0 minutes
Nutritional Info: 125.7 Cal; 11 g Fats; 1.3 g Protein; 1.7 g Net Carb; 3.7 g Fiber;
Ingredients
- 1 avocado, pitted, sliced
- 4 ounces chopped lettuce
- 4 tablespoons chopped chives
- ½ of a lime, juiced
- 2 tablespoons olive oil

Extra:
- 1/8 teaspoon salt
- 1/8 teaspoon ground black pepper

Directions
- Prepare the dressing and for this, take a small bowl, add oil, lime juice, salt, and black

pepper, stir until mixed, and then slowly mix oil until combined.
- Take a large bowl, add avocado, lettuce, and chives, and then toss gently.
- Drizzle with dressing, toss until well coated, and then serve.

Dinner – Chili-glazed Salmon

Serving: 2
Preparation time: 5 minutes; Cooking time: 10 minutes
Nutritional Info: 112.5 Cal; 5.6 g Fats; 12 g Protein; 3.4 g Net Carb; 0 g Fiber;
Ingredients
- 2 salmon fillets
- 2 tablespoons sweet chili sauce
- 2 teaspoons chopped chives
- ½ teaspoon sesame seeds

Directions
- Switch on the oven, then set it to 400 degrees F and let it preheat.

until combined, and serve.

- Add grilled chicken in it, toss

- Meanwhile, place salmon in a shallow dish, add chili sauce and chives and toss until mixed.
- Transfer prepared salmon

onto a baking sheet lined with parchment sheet, drizzle with remaining sauce and bake for 10 minutes until

thoroughly cooked.
- Garnish with sesame seeds and serve straight away.

Day 48
Breakfast – Crepe

Serving: 2
Preparation time: 5 minutes; Cooking time: 9 minutes
Nutritional Info: 118 Cal; 9.4 g Fats; 6.5 g Protein; 1 g Net Carb; 0.9 g Fiber;
Ingredients
- 2/3 tablespoon psyllium husk
- 1 1/3 tablespoon cream cheese
- 2 eggs
- 1 egg white
- 1 tablespoon unsalted butter
Directions
- Prepare the batter and for this, place all the ingredients in a bowl, except for butter, and then whisk by using a stick blender until smooth and very liquid.
- Take a skillet pan, place it over medium heat, add ½

tablespoon butter and when it melts, pour in half of the batter, spread evenly, and cook until the top has firmed.
- Carefully flip the crepe, then continue cooking for 2 minutes until cooked and then transfer it to a plate.
- Add remaining butter and when it melts, cook another crepe in the same manner and then serve.

Lunch – Spinach and Bacon Salad

Serving: 2
Preparation time: 5 minutes; Cooking time: 5 minutes
Nutritional Info: 181.5 Cal; 16.7 g Fats; 7.3 g

Protein; 0.2 g Net Carb; 0.3 g Fiber;
Ingredients
- 4 ounces spinach
- 4 sliced of bacon, chopped
- 2 eggs, boiled, sliced
- ¼ cup mayonnaise
Directions
- Take a skillet pan, place it over medium heat, add bacon, and cook for 5 minutes until browned.
- Meanwhile, take a salad bowl, add spinach in it, top with bacon and eggs and drizzle with mayonnaise.
- Toss until well mixed and then serve.

Dinner – Taco Lime Grilled Chicken

Serving: 2

Preparation time: 5 minutes; Cooking time: 12 minutes
Nutritional Info: 128.3 Cal; 9 g Fats; 11.6 g Protein; 0.3 g Net Carb; 0 g Fiber;
Ingredients
- 2 chicken thighs, boneless
- ½ of a lime, juiced
- 1 ½ teaspoon taco seasoning
- 1 tablespoon olive oil

Directions

- Prepare the marinade and for this, take a small bowl, add lemon juice and taco seasoning and stir until mixed.
- Brush chicken with prepared marinade and then marinate for 15 minutes.
- Then take a grill pan, place it over medium-high heat, grease it with oil and when

hot, add marinated chicken and cook for 5 minutes per side until thoroughly cooked.
- When done, transfer chicken to a cutting board, let it cool for 5 minutes, then cut the chicken into slices and serve.

Day 49

Breakfast – Breakfast Burgers with Avocado

Serving: 2
Preparation time: 5 minutes; Cooking time: 15 minutes
Nutritional Info: 205.2 Cal; 18.5 g Fats; 7.7 g Protein; 0.7 g Net Carb; 1.9 g Fiber;
Ingredients
- 4 strips of bacon
- 2 tablespoons chopped lettuce
- 2 avocados
- 2 eggs
- 2 tablespoons mayonnaise

Extra:
- ¼ teaspoon salt
- ¼ teaspoon sesame seeds

Directions

- Take a skillet pan, place it over medium heat and when hot, add bacon strips and cook for 5 minutes until crispy.
- Transfer bacon to a plate lined with paper towels, crack an egg into the pan, and cook for 2 to 4 minutes or until fried to the desired level; fry remaining egg in the same manner.
- Prepare sandwiches and for this, cut each avocado in half widthwise, remove the pit, and scoop out the flesh.
- Fill the hollow of two avocado

halves with mayonnaise, then top each half with 1 tablespoon of chopped lettuce, 2 bacon strips, and a fried egg, and then cover with the second half of avocado.
- Sprinkle sesame seeds on avocados and serve.

Lunch – Teriyaki Chicken

Serving: 2
Preparation time: 5 minutes; Cooking time: 18 minutes

Nutritional Info: 150 Cal; 9 g Fats; 17.3 g Protein; 0 g Net Carb; 0 g Fiber;

Ingredients

- 2 chicken thighs, boneless
- 2 tablespoons soy sauce
- 1 tablespoon swerve sweetener
- 1 tablespoon olive oil

Directions

- Take a skillet pan, place it over medium heat, add oil and when hot, add chicken thighs and cook for 5 minutes per side until seared.
- Then sprinkle sugar over chicken thighs, drizzle with soy sauce and bring the sauce to boil.
- Switch heat to medium-low level, continue cooking for 3 minutes until chicken is evenly glazed, and then transfer to a plate.
- Serve chicken with cauliflower rice.

Dinner –Cardamom Salmon

Serving: 2

Preparation time: 5 minutes; Cooking time: 20 minutes

Nutritional Info: 143.3 Cal; 10.7 g Fats; 11.8 g Protein; 0 g Net Carb; 0 g Fiber;

Ingredients

- 2 salmon fillets
- ¾ teaspoon salt
- 2/3 tablespoon ground cardamom
- 1 tablespoon liquid stevia
- 1 ½ tablespoon olive oil

Directions

- Switch on the oven, then set it to 275 degrees F and let it preheat.
- Meanwhile, prepare the sauce and for this, place oil in a small bowl, and whisk in cardamom and stevia until combined.
- Take a baking dish, place salmon in it, brush with prepared sauce on all sides, and let it marinate for 20 minutes at room temperature.
- Then season salmon with salt and bake for 15 to 20 minutes until thoroughly cooked.
- When done, flake salmon with two forks and then serve.

Shopping List for Week 8

Remaining foods from the previous week(s):
- 4 ounces Tri0color Cole Slaw
- 2 ounces whipped cream
- 1 egg
- 6 ounces of turkey bacon
- 3 ounces chopped lettuce
- 4 tablespoons tomato sauce

Look in pantry for:
- Minced garlic
- Whole garlic cloves
- Basil leaves
- Himalayan pink salt/sea salt

- Organic black pepper
- Organic dried rosemary
- Organic dried oregano
- Organic dried basil
- Organic paprika
- Organic crushed red pepper
- Organic ground cumin
- Organic Italian seasoning
- Baking powder
- Nutritional yeast
- Soy sauce, low-sodium
- Apple cider vinegar
- Avocado oil
- Olive oil
- Butter
- Mayonnaise

Purchase the following:

Items:	Store:	Quantity:	Price:
Coconut flour, 16 oz.	Walmart	1	3.12
Zucchini, 3 count	Walmart	1	1.24
Ground turkey	Walmart	1	1.5
Large White Eggs, 6 count, 12 ounce	Walmart	3	1.78
Spinach, 10 oz.	Walmart	1	1.23
Broccoli and cauliflower florets, 12 oz.	Walmart	1	1
Feta cheese 5 oz.	Walmart	1	2.1
Green Beans, 14.5 oz.	Walmart	1	0.5
Chicken Sausage in Chicken Broth, 8.2 oz.	Walmart	1	1.54
Boneless Skinless Chicken thighs, 2.5 lb. 6 count	Walmart	1	3.6
Cream cheese 12 oz.	Walmart	1	0.8
Shredded Mozzarella Cheese, 8 oz.	Walmart	1	1.54
Lime	Walmart	1	0.16
Tuna in Water, 5 oz.	Walmart	1	0.81
		Total:	19.48

Day 50

Breakfast – Keto Bread

Serving: 2
Preparation time: 5 minutes; Cooking time: 10 minutes
Nutritional Info: 235 Cal; 20 g Fats; 8 g Protein; 3.7 g Net Carb; 3 g Fiber;
Ingredients
- 2 2/3 tablespoons coconut flour
- 2 tablespoons avocado oil
- 1 teaspoon baking powder
- 2 eggs
- 1/8 teaspoon salt

Directions
- Switch on the oven, then set it to 375 degrees F and let it preheat.
- Meanwhile, prepare the batter for this, add all the ingredients in a bowl and then whisk until well combined.
- Take a 4 by 4 inches heatproof baking pan, grease it with oil, pour in the prepared batter and bake 10 minutes until bread is firm.
- When done, let the bread cool in the pan for 5 minutes, then transfer it to a wire rack and cool for 20 minutes.
- Slice the bread and then serve.

Lunch – Keto Pasta

Serving: 2
Preparation time: 40 minutes; Cooking time: 7 minutes
Nutritional Info: 218.3 Cal; 16.5 g Fats; 15.3 g Protein; 2 g Net Carb; 2.2 g Fiber;
Ingredients
- 4 ounces grated mozzarella cheese
- 2 egg yolks
- 2 tablespoons tomato sauce

Extra:
- ¼ teaspoon salt
- ¼ teaspoon ground black pepper

Directions
- Take a heatproof bowl, add mozzarella in it, and microwave for 2 minutes or until it melts.
- Whisk in yolks until combined, take a baking dish lined with parchment paper, and add cheese mixture in it.
- Cover the cheese mixture with another parchment paper, press and spread the cheese mixture as thinly as possible, let it rest for 10 minutes until slightly firm.
- Then uncover it, cut out thin spaghetti by using a knife and refrigerate the pasta for 45 minutes.
- When ready to cook, take a saucepan half full with salty water, bring it to boil, add pasta and cook for 5 minutes until spaghetti is tender.
- Drain the spaghetti, distribute it between two bowls, top with tomato sauce, season with salt and black pepper, toss until well mixed, and then serve.

Dinner – Chicken with Cauliflower Rice

Serving: 2
Preparation time: 5 minutes; Cooking time: 15 minutes
Nutritional Info: 185 Cal; 14 g Fats; 12.5 g Protein; 1.9 g Net Carb; 0.4 g Fiber;
Ingredients
- 3 ounces cauliflower florets, grated
- 1 chicken thigh, boneless, diced
- 1 teaspoon soy sauce
- 1 teaspoon apple cider vinegar
- 1 tablespoon grated mozzarella cheese

Extra:
- 1/3 teaspoon salt
- 1/3 teaspoon ground black pepper
- ¼ teaspoon dried rosemary
- 2 tablespoons olive oil

Directions
- Take a skillet pan, place it over medium heat, add 1 tablespoon oil in it and when hot, add chicken pieces and cook for 3 minutes.
- Then drizzle with soy sauce and vinegar, season with ¼ teaspoon salt and black pepper, toss until mixed and cook for 5 minutes until nicely golden and cooked through.
- When done, transfer chicken to a plate, add remaining oil in the pan, and when hot, add cauliflower.
- Season cauliflower with salt and black pepper, toss until mixed and cook for 4 minutes until cooked.
- Return chicken into the pan, toss until mixed and then cook for 1 minute until hot.
- Sprinkle with cheese, cook for 1 minute until cheese melts, and then serve.

Day 51

Breakfast – Omelet with Meat

Serving: 2
Preparation time: 5 minutes; Cooking time: 12 minutes
Nutritional Info: 126.3 Cal; 8.6 g Fats; 10.7 g Protein; 1.5 g Net Carb; 0 g Fiber;
Ingredients
- 2 ounces ground turkey
- 1 tablespoon chopped spinach
- 1 tablespoon whipped topping
- 2 eggs
- 2 tablespoons grated mozzarella cheese

Extra:
- ¼ teaspoon salt
- 1/8 teaspoon ground black pepper

Directions
- Take a skillet pan, place it over medium heat, add ground turkey and cook for 5 minutes until cooked through.
- Meanwhile, crack eggs in a bowl, add whipped topping and

spinach and whisk until combined.

- When the meat is cooked, transfer it to a plate, then switch heat to the low level and pour in the egg mixture.
- Cook the eggs for 3 minutes until the bottom is firm, then flip it and cook for 3 minutes until the omelet is firmed, covering the pan.
- Sprinkle cheese on the omelet, cook for 1 minute until cheese has melted, and then slide omelet to a plate.
- Spread ground meat on the omelet, roll it, then cut it in half and serve.

Lunch – Spicy Sautéed Green Beans

Serving: 2
Preparation time: 5 minutes; Cooking time: 10 minutes
Nutritional Info: 108.5 Cal; 10.1 g Fats; 0.5 g Protein; 2.2 g Net Carb; 1.6 g Fiber;
Ingredients

- 4 ounces green beans

- ½ teaspoon minced garlic
- ¼ teaspoon crushed red pepper
- 1 ½ tablespoon olive oil

Extra:

- 1/3 teaspoon salt
- ¼ teaspoon ground black pepper

Directions

- Take a saucepan half full with salted water, place it over medium heat, bring the water to boil, then add green beans and cook for 4 minutes until tender.
- Drain the beans, wipe the pan, return it over medium heat, add oil and when hot, add garlic and cook for 1 minute until fragrant.
- Then add green beans, season with salt and black pepper, cook for 1 minute and transfer beans to a plate.
- Sprinkle red pepper on the green beans and serve.

Dinner – Turkey Spinach Sliders

Serving: 2
Preparation time: 5 minutes; Cooking time: 10 minutes
Nutritional Info: 240 Cal; 20 g Fats; 14.4 g Protein; 0.3 g Net Carb; 0.4 g Fiber;
Ingredients

- 2 tablespoons chopped spinach
- ½ teaspoon minced garlic
- 3 ounces ground turkey
- 1 ½ tablespoon olive oil
- 2 ounces chopped lettuce

Extra:

- 1/3 teaspoon salt
- 1/3 teaspoon ground black pepper
- ¼ teaspoon ground cumin

Directions

- Take a bowl, place all the ingredients in it, except for oil and lettuce, stir until combined, and then shape the mixture into two patties.
- Take a skillet pan, place it over medium heat, add oil and when hot, add patties and cook for 5 minutes per side until cooked.

- Serve patties with chopped lettuce.

Day 52
Breakfast – Pancakes

Serving: 2
Preparation time: 5 minutes; Cooking time: 6 minutes
Nutritional Info: 166.8 Cal; 15 g Fats; 5.8 g Protein; 1.8 g Net Carb; 0.8 g Fiber;
Ingredients
6. ¼ cup almond flour
7. 1 ½ tablespoon unsalted butter
8. 2 ounces cream cheese, softened
9. 2 eggs
Directions
- Take a bowl, crack eggs in it, whisk well until fluffy, and then whisk in flour and cream cheese until well combined.
- Take a skillet pan, place it over medium heat, add butter and when it melts, drop pancake batter in four sections, spread it evenly, and cook for 2 minutes per side until brown.
- Serve straight away.

Lunch – Chili Lime Chicken with Coleslaw

Serving: 2
Preparation time: 35 minutes; Cooking time: 8 minutes
Nutritional Info: 157.3 Cal; 12.8 g Fats; 9 g Protein; 1 g Net Carb; 0.5 g Fiber;
Ingredients
1. 1 chicken thigh, boneless
2. 2 ounces coleslaw
3. ¼ teaspoon minced garlic
4. ¾ tablespoon apple cider vinegar
5. ½ of a lime, juiced, zested
Extra:
6. ¼ teaspoon paprika
7. ¼ teaspoon salt
8. 2 tablespoons olive oil
9. 1 tablespoon unsalted butter
Directions
- Prepare the marinade and for this, take a medium bowl, add vinegar, oil, garlic, paprika, salt, lime juice, and zest and stir until well mixed.
- Cut chicken thighs into bite-size pieces, toss until well mixed, and marinate it in the refrigerator for 30 minutes.
- Then take a skillet pan, place it over medium-high heat, add butter and marinated chicken pieces and cook for 8 minutes until golden brown and thoroughly cooked.
- Serve chicken with coleslaw.

Dinner – Sausage and Vegetable Soup

Serving: 2
Preparation time: 5 minutes; Cooking time: 25 minutes
Nutritional Info: 222.5 Cal; 16.8 g Fats; 11.7 g Protein; 4.6 g Net Carb; 2.1 g Fiber;
Ingredients

- 4 ounces chicken sausage, sliced, cooked
- 3 ounces green beans, diced
- 2 ounces chopped spinach
- 1 ounce chopped cauliflower florets
- 1 ounce chopped broccoli florets

Extra:

- 1/3 teaspoon salt
- ¼ teaspoon ground black pepper
- ¼ teaspoon paprika
- 1 ½ tablespoon olive oil
- 1 ½ cup water

Directions

- Take a saucepan, place it over medium heat, pour in water and sausage, and bring the mixture to boil.
- Then continue boiling for 3 minutes, then remaining ingredients, stir, and simmer the soup for 20 minutes until sausage and vegetables are cooked.
- Ladle soup into bowls and serve.

Day 53
Breakfast – Zucchini and Broccoli Fritters

Serving: 2
Preparation time: 10 minutes; Cooking time: 10 minutes
Nutritional Info: 191 Cal; 16.6 g Fats; 9.6 g Protein; 0.8 g Net Carb; 0.2 g Fiber;
Ingredients

- 1 ounce chopped broccoli
- 1 zucchini, grated, squeezed
- 2 eggs
- 2 tablespoons almond flour
- ½ teaspoon nutritional yeast

Extra:

- 1/3 teaspoon salt
- ¼ teaspoon dried basil
- 1 tablespoon olive oil

Directions

- Wrap grated zucchini in a cheesecloth, twist it well to remove excess moisture, and then place zucchini in a bowl.
- Add remaining ingredients, except for oil, and then whisk well until combined.
- Take a skillet pan, place it over medium heat, add oil and when hot, drop zucchini mixture in four portions, shape them into flat patties and cook for 4 minutes per side until thoroughly cooked.
- Serve straight away.

Lunch – Tuna and Spinach Salad

Serving: 2
Preparation time: 5 minutes; Cooking time: 0 minutes
Nutritional Info: 191 Cal; 16.6 g Fats; 9.6 g Protein; 0.8 g Net Carb; 0.2 g Fiber;

Ingredients

1. 4 ounces tuna, packed in water
2. 2 ounces chopped spinach
3. 1 tablespoon grated mozzarella cheese
4. 1/3 cup mayonnaise

Extra:

5. ¼ teaspoon salt
6. 1/8 teaspoon ground black pepper

Directions

- Take a bowl, add mayonnaise in it along with cheese, season with salt and black pepper and whisk until combined.
- Then add tuna and spinach, toss until mixed and serve.

Dinner – Garlic Chicken with Mozzarella

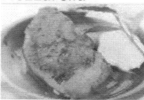

Serving: 2
Preparation time: 5 minutes; Cooking time: 10 minutes
Nutritional Info: 100 Cal; 100 g Fats; 100 g Protein; 100 g Net Carb; 100 g Fiber;

Ingredients

- 2 chicken thighs, boneless
- 4 basil leaves, chopped
- 2 cloves of garlic, peeled, sliced
- 2 tablespoons olive oil
- 1 tablespoon grated mozzarella cheese

Extra:

- 1/3 teaspoon salt

- 1/3 teaspoon ground black pepper
- ½ teaspoon dried oregano

Directions

- Prepare chicken thighs and for this, create a pocket into each chicken thigh and then place them in a baking dish.
- Stuff chicken with basil and garlic, drizzle with oil, season with salt, black pepper, and oregano and bake for 8 minutes or until chicken is almost cooked.
- Then sprinkle cheese on top of each chicken, continue baking for 2 minutes until cheese has melted and the top is browned, and serve.

Day 54

Breakfast – Zucchini Breakfast Hash

Serving: 2

Preparation time: 5 minutes; Cooking time: 15 minutes
Nutritional Info: 144.5 Cal; 12.5 g Fats; 6 g Protein; 0.9 g Net Carb; 0.5 g Fiber;

Ingredients

- 4 slices of bacon, chopped
- 1 zucchini, diced
- 2 eggs

- 2 tablespoons olive oil

Extra:

- 3/4 teaspoon salt, divided
- ¼ teaspoon ground black pepper

Directions

- Take a skillet pan, place it over medium heat,

add bacon, and cook for 5 minutes until lightly brown.

- Then add zucchini, season with ½ teaspoon salt, stir, cook for 10 minutes and then transfer to plate.
- Fry eggs to desired level in olive oil, season eggs with salt and black pepper to taste and serve with zucchini hash.

Lunch – Beans and Sausage

Serving: 2
Preparation time: 5 minutes; Cooking time: 4 minutes
Nutritional Info: 182 Cal; 13.3 g Fats; 10.9 g Protein; 3.5 g Net Carb; 1.6 g Fiber;
Ingredients

- 4 ounces chicken sausage, sliced
- 4 ounces green beans
- ¼ teaspoon dried oregano

- 1 tablespoon olive oil
- 1 cup of water

Extra:
- ½ teaspoon salt
- ½ teaspoon ground black pepper
- ¼ teaspoon dried basil

Directions
- Switch on the instant pot, place all the ingredients in the inner pot, stir and shut with lid.
- Press the manual button, cook for 4 minutes at high-pressure setting, and, when done, do quick pressure release.
- Serve straight away.

Dinner – Buttery Turkey and Broccoli

Serving: 2
Preparation time: 5 minutes; Cooking time: 8 minutes
Nutritional Info: 315 Cal; 27 g Fats; 15.8 g Protein; 1.9 g Net Carb; 1.4 g Fiber;
Ingredients

- 3 ounces broccoli florets
- 4 ounces ground turkey
- 3 tablespoons unsalted butter
- ½ teaspoon dried rosemary
- 2 tablespoons water

Extra:
- ¼ teaspoon salt
- 1/8 teaspoon ground black pepper

Directions
- Take a heatproof bowl, place broccoli florets in it, cover it with plastic wrap, poke some holes in it with a fork and microwave for 2 minutes until steamed.
- Meanwhile, take a skillet pan, place it over medium heat, add turkey and butter and cook for 3 minutes.
- Then season the turkey with salt, black pepper, and rosemary and continue cooking for 5 minutes until cooked and browned.
- Serve turkey with steamed broccoli florets.

Day 55

Breakfast – Meat Bagels

Serving: 2
Preparation time: 5 minutes; Cooking time: 20 minutes
Nutritional Info: 100 Cal; 100 g Fats; 100 g Protein; 100 g Net Carb; 100 g Fiber;
Ingredients

- 4 ounces ground turkey
- 1 slice of bacon, chopped
- 1 egg
- 2 tablespoons tomato sauce
- 2 ounces coleslaw

Extra:

- ½ teaspoon paprika
- ½ teaspoon salt
- ¼ teaspoon ground black pepper
- 1 tablespoon unsalted butter, softened

Directions

- Switch on the oven, then set it to 400 degrees F and let it preheat.
- Meanwhile, take a bowl, place all the ingredients in it, mix well, and then shape the mixture into two bagels.
- Place bagels into a baking dish, bake for 20 minutes until cooked through, and when done, let them cool for 10 minutes.
- Slice the bagel, fill with coleslaw, and serve.

Lunch – Bacon Wrapped Cream Cheese Stuffed Zucchini

Serving: 2
Preparation time: 5 minutes; Cooking time: 20 minutes
Nutritional Info: 198.8 Cal; 17.2 g Fats; 8.4 g Protein; 1.7 g Net Carb; 0.8 g Fiber;
Ingredients

- 1 zucchini, halved lengthwise
- 3 tablespoons cream cheese
- 1 tablespoon chopped spinach
- 1 tablespoon grated mozzarella cheese
- 2 slices of bacon

Extra:

- ¼ teaspoon salt
- 1/8 teaspoon ground black pepper
- 1/8 teaspoon crushed red pepper

Directions

- Switch on the oven, then set it to 350 degrees F and let it preheat.
- Meanwhile, cut zucchini into half lengthwise, then use a spoon to remove the seedy center and set aside until required.
- Place remaining ingredients, except for bacon in a bowl, stir well, and then evenly stuffed this mixture into zucchini.
- Wrap each zucchini half with a bacon slice, place them on a baking sheet lined with parchment paper and cook for 15 to 20 minutes until zucchini is tender and bacon is browned.
- Serve straight away.

Dinner – Basil Stuffed Chicken

Serving: 2
Preparation time: 10 minutes; Cooking time: 20 minutes

Nutritional Info: 263.5 Cal; 19.9 g Fats; 19.8 g Protein; 101.30 g Net Carb; 0 g Fiber;

Ingredients

- 2 chicken thighs, boneless
- ¼ teaspoon minced garlic
- 1 teaspoon dried basil
- 2 tablespoons cream cheese
- 2 tablespoons grated mozzarella cheese

Extra:

- ¼ teaspoon ground black pepper
- ¼ teaspoon salt
- 1 tablespoon olive oil

Directions

- Switch on the oven, then set it to 375 degrees F and let it preheat.
- Meanwhile, take a bowl, add garlic, basil, cream cheese, mozzarella, and black pepper and stir until mixed.
- Make a pocket into each chicken with a knife, stuffed it evenly with prepared mixture, place chicken into a baking dish, drizzle with oil, season with salt, and bake for 15 to 20 minutes until chicken is thoroughly cooked.
- Serve straight away.

Day 56
Breakfast – Breastfast Omelet Sandwich

Serving: 2
Preparation time: 10 minutes; Cooking time: 20 minutes
Nutritional Info: 377 Cal; 32.3 g Fats; 15.1 g Protein; 3.2 g Net Carb; 3.4 g Fiber;

Ingredients

1. 2 2/3 tablespoons coconut flour
2. 1 teaspoon baking powder
3. 3 tablespoons avocado oil
4. 3 eggs
5. 2 egg whites

Extra:

6. ¼ teaspoon salt
7. 1/8 teaspoon ground black pepper
8. 1/8 teaspoon paprika

Directions

- Switch on the oven, then set it to 375 degrees F and let it preheat.
- Meanwhile, prepare the batter for this, add flour, 2 tablespoons avocado oil, baking powder, 2 eggs, and 1/8 teaspoon in a bowl and then whisk until well combined.
- Take a 4 by 4 inches heatproof baking pan, grease it with oil, pour in the prepared batter and bake 10 minutes until bread is firm.
- Meanwhile, prepare omelet and for this, crack the remaining egg in a bowl, add egg whites, black pepper, paprika, and remaining salt and whisk until combined.
- Take a skillet pan, place it over medium heat, add oil and when hot, pour in egg mixture, cook for 2 minutes, then

flip it and continue cooking for 2 minutes until done, set aside until required.

- When done, let the bread cool in the pan for 5 minutes, then transfer it to a wire rack and cool for 20 minutes.
- Cut bread into four slices, divide omelet into two, sandwich it between bread slices and serve.

Lunch – Spinach Salad with Feta Dressing

Serving: 2
Preparation time: 5 minutes; Cooking time: 3 minutes
Nutritional Info: 204.3 Cal; 19.5 g Fats; 5.1 g Protein; 1.7 g Net Carb; 0.8 g Fiber;
Ingredients
- 4 ounces of spinach leaves
- 3 tablespoons olive oil

- 3 ounces feta cheese, crumbled
- 1 ½ tablespoon apple cider vinegar

Extra:
- 1/8 teaspoon salt
- 1/8 teaspoon ground black pepper

Directions
- Take a skillet pan, place it over medium heat, add oil and when warmed, add cheese, cook for 1 minute until cheese has slightly melted and then stir in vinegar; remove the pan from heat.
- Take a bowl, add spinach in it, top with feta cheese mixture and toss until mixed.
- Serve straight away.

Dinner – Meatloaf

Serving: 2
Preparation time: 5 minutes; Cooking time: 4 minutes
Nutritional Info: 196.5 Cal; 13.5 g Fats; 18.7 g

Protein; 18.7 g Net Carb; 0 g Fiber;
Ingredients
- 4 ounces ground turkey
- 1 egg
- 1 tablespoon grated mozzarella cheese
- ¼ teaspoon Italian seasoning
- ½ tablespoon soy sauce

Extra:
- ¼ teaspoon salt
- 1/8 teaspoon ground black pepper

Directions
- Take a bowl, place all the ingredients in it, and stir until mixed.
- Take a heatproof mug, spoon in prepared mixture and microwave for 3 minutes at high heat setting until cooked.
- When done, let meatloaf rest in the mug for 1 minute, then take it out, cut it into two slices and serve.

Week 9

<u>Shopping List for Week 9</u>

Remaining foods from the previous
week(s):
- 1 ounce chopped lettuce
- 12 oz. Coconut flour
- 3 oz. green beans
- 8 oz. cream cheese
- 2 oz. turkey bacon
- 1 oz. tuna, packed in water
- 2 ounces whipped cream

Look in pantry for:
- Garlic
- Coffee
- Himalayan pink salt/sea salt

- Organic black pepper
- Organic ground cumin
- Organic paprika
- Organic Cajun seasoning
- Organic red chili flakes
- Organic curry powder
- Organic dried cilantro
- Psyllium husk powder
- Sriracha sauce
- Vanilla extract, unsweetened
- Olive oil
- Coconut oil
- Butter
- Mayonnaise
- Greek yogurt

Purchase the following:

Items:	Store:	Quantity:	Price:
Zucchini, 2 count	Walmart	1	1.6
Large White Eggs, 12 count	Walmart	1	1.38
Spinach 10 oz.	Walmart	1	1.23
Feta cheese 5 oz.	Walmart	1	2.1
Boneless Skinless Chicken thighs, 2.5 lb. 6 count	Walmart	2	5.6
Mozzarella Cheese, 8 oz. block	Walmart	1	1.54
Tuna in Water, 5 oz. Can	Walmart	2	0.81
Lime	Walmart	1	0.16
Hass Avocado, 3 Count	Walmart	1	1.5
Roma Tomato, 1 Count	Walmart	1	0.16
Green Olives Stuffed with Minced Pimento, 7 oz.	Walmart	1	1
Green Cabbage, 1 lb.	Walmart	1	0.58
Scallion, 1 bunch	Walmart	1	0.5
Coconut milk cream of coconut 15 oz.	Walmart	1	1.64
		Total:	19.8

Day 57

Breakfast – Butter coffee

Serving: 2
Preparation time: 5 minutes; Cooking time: 0 minutes;
Nutritional Info: 334 Cal; 38 g Fats; 1 g Protein; 0 g Net Carb; 0 g Fiber;
Ingredients

- 2 cups brewed coffee, hot
- 4 tablespoons butter, unsalted
- 2 tablespoons coconut oil

Directions

- Place all the ingredients in a food processor or blender in the order and then pulse for 1 minute until smooth.
- Distribute coffee evenly between two cups and then serve.

Lunch – Tuna and Spinach Salad

Serving: 2
Preparation time: 5 minutes; Cooking time: 10 minutes;
Nutritional Info: 398.5 Cal; 15.5 g Fats; 62.8 g Protein; 0.7 g Net Carb; 1.3 g Fiber;
Ingredients

- 2 ounces of spinach leaves
- 2 ounces tuna, packed in water
- ¼ teaspoon ground black pepper
- 1/4 teaspoon sea salt
- 2 tablespoons coconut oil, melted

Directions

- Take a salad bowl, place spinach leaves in it, drizzle with 1 tablespoon oil, sprinkle with 1/8 teaspoon of salt and black pepper, and then toss until mixed.
- Top with tuna, sprinkle with remaining salt and black pepper, drizzle with oil and then serve.

Dinner – Paprika Chicken with Lime

Serving: 2
Preparation time: 1 hour and 5 minutes; Cooking time: 10 minutes;
Nutritional Info: 212.5 Cal; 7.3 g Fats; 35.6 g Protein; 0.6 g Net Carb; 0.5 g Fiber;
Ingredients

- 2 chicken thighs, pasteurized
- ½ of a lime, juiced, zested
- 1/3 teaspoon ground cumin
- ½ teaspoon paprika
- 1 cup of water

Extra:

- 1/3 teaspoon salt
- ¼ teaspoon ground black pepper

Directions

- Take a small bowl, add lime juice, lime zest, paprika, salt, and black pepper and then stir until combined.
- Brush this spice mixture thoroughly on all sides of chicken thighs, place chicken into a bowl, cover with a plastic wrap and then let it marinate for a minimum of 1 hour.
- When ready to cook, plug in the instant pot, pour water into the inner pot, insert a steamer rack, and place chicken on it.
- Shut with lid, press the "manual" button, then cook the chicken for 10 minutes, and when done, do quick pressure release.
- Transfer chicken to a plate,

reserve the broth for later use and

Day 58

Breakfast – Bacon, Avocado Egg Boats

Serving: 2
Preparation time: 5 minutes; Cooking time: 15 minutes;
Nutritional Info: 229 Cal; 18 g Fats; 11 g Protein; 1.1 g Net Carb; 4.6 g Fiber;
Ingredients
- 1 avocado, pitted
- 2 slices of turkey bacon, pasteurized
- 2 eggs pasteurized

Extra:
- ¼ teaspoon salt
- 1/8 teaspoon ground black pepper

Directions
- Switch on the oven, then set it to 425 degrees F and let it preheat.
- Meanwhile, prepare the avocado and for this, cut the avocado into half, remove the pit and then scoop out some of the flesh to make the hollow bigger.
- Take a skillet pan, place it over medium heat and when hot, add bacon slices and

serve chicken straight away.

cook for 3 minutes per side until crisp.
- Transfer each slice into the hollow of each avocado half, crack the egg into each hollow and bake the egg boats for 12 to 15 minutes until the egg has cooked to the desired level.
- When done, season egg boats with salt and black pepper and serve.

Lunch – Italian Keto Plate

Serving: 2
Preparation time: 5 minutes; Cooking time: 0 minutes;
Nutritional Info: 412 Cal; 35 g Fats; 20 g Protein; 4 g Net Carb; 1.5 g Fiber;
Ingredients
- 2 ounces fresh mozzarella cheese, sliced
- 2 ounces tuna, packed in water
- 1 Roma tomato, halved
- 1/4 cup olive oil
- 8 green olives

Extra:
- ¼ teaspoon salt

- 1/8 teaspoon ground black pepper

Directions
- Take two serving plates and then distribute tomato, cheese, and tuna evenly between them.
- Season with salt and black pepper and then serve with olive oil.

Dinner – Creamy Tuna, Spinach, and Eggs Plates

Serving: 2
Preparation time: 5 minutes; Cooking time: 0 minutes;
Nutritional Info: 212 Cal; 14.1 g Fats; 18 g Protein; 1.9 g Net Carb; 1.3 g Fiber;
Ingredients
- 2 ounces of spinach leaves
- 2 ounces tuna, packed in water
- 2 pasteurized eggs, boiled
- 4 tablespoons cream cheese, full-fat

Extra:
- ¼ teaspoon salt

- 1/8 teaspoon ground black pepper

Directions
- Take two plates and evenly distribute spinach

and tuna between them.
- Peel the eggs, cut them into half, divide them between the plates and then

season with salt and black pepper.
- Serve with cream cheese.

Day 59

Breakfast – Coconut Cream Berries

Serving: 2
Preparation time: 5 minutes; Cooking time: 0 minutes;
Nutritional Info: 213 Cal; 21 g Fats; 2.5 g Protein; 4.5 g Net Carb; 2 g Fiber;
Ingredients
- 4 ounces fresh strawberries
- 2 teaspoons vanilla extract, unsweetened
- 1 tablespoon coconut oil
- 4 ounces coconut cream, full-fat

Directions
- Take a large bowl, place all the ingredients in it and then mix by using an immersion blender until smooth.
- Distribute evenly between two bowls and then serve.

Lunch – Chicken with Green Beans and Spinach

Serving: 2
Preparation time: 5 minutes; Cooking time: 18 minutes;
Nutritional Info: 444 Cal; 37.5 g Fats; 22.2 g Protein; 2.6 g Net Carb; 1.8 g Fiber;
Ingredients
- 2 ounces spinach leaves
- 3 ounces green beans
- 2 chicken thighs, pasteurized
- 2 tablespoons butter, unsalted
- 4 tablespoons mayonnaise, full-fat

Extra:
- 1/3 teaspoon salt
- 1/8 teaspoon ground black pepper

Directions
- Take a frying pan, place it over

medium heat, add 1 tablespoon butter and wait until it melts.
- Season chicken with salt and black pepper, add to the frying pan and then cook for 4 to 5 minutes per side until golden brown and thoroughly cooked.
- Add remaining butter, then green beans and fry them for 3 to 4 minutes until tender-crisp.
- Add spinach, toss until mixed, and continue frying for 2 minutes until spinach leaves wilts.
- Distribute chicken and vegetables between two plates and then serve with mayonnaise.

Dinner – Cajun Chicken

Serving: 2
Preparation time: 5 minutes; Cooking time: 10 minutes;
Nutritional Info: 225 Cal; 16 g Fats; 20.1 g Protein; 0.6 g Net Carb; 0 g Fiber;

Ingredients
- 2 chicken thighs, pasteurized
- 1 tablespoon Cajun seasoning
- 2 tablespoons butter, unsalted, melted

Directions
- Take a small bowl, add butter in it, stir in Cajun seasoning and then brush this mixture on all sides of chicken.
- Take a griddle pan, place it over medium-high heat, grease it with oil and when hot, add prepared chicken thighs, and then grill for 5 minutes per side until thoroughly cooked.
- Serve straight away.

Day 60
Breakfast – Chaffles

Serving: 2
Preparation time: 5 minutes; Cooking time: 10 minutes;
Nutritional Info: 142 Cal; 9.8 g Fats; 10.3 g Protein; 2.3 g Net Carb; 1 g Fiber;
Ingredients
1. 2 teaspoons coconut flour
2. ½ cup shredded mozzarella cheese, full-fat
3. 1 egg, pasteurized

Directions
- Switch on a mini waffle maker and let it preheat for 5 minutes.
- Meanwhile, take a medium bowl, place all the ingredients in it and then mix by using an immersion blender until smooth.
- Ladle the batter evenly into the waffle maker, shut with lid, and let it cook for 3 to 4 minutes until firm and golden brown.
- Serve straight away.

Lunch – Cheese and Bacon Balls

Serving: 2
Preparation time: 10 minutes; Cooking time: 8 minutes;
Nutritional Info: 137 Cal; 13 g Fats; 5.5 g Protein; 1 g Net Carb; 0 g Fiber;
Ingredients
1. 2 slices of bacon, pasteurized
2. 1 ¼ tablespoon butter, unsalted
3. 1 ¼ ounces cream cheese, full-fat
4. 1 ¼ ounces shredded mozzarella cheese, full-fat
5. 1/8 teaspoon red chili flakes

Directions
- Take a frying pan, place it over medium heat and when hot, add bacon slices and cook for 3 minutes per side until crisp.

- Transfer bacon slices to a cutting board, let them cool for 5 minutes, chop them, then transfer chopped bacon into a medium bowl and set aside until required.
- Take a shallow dish, add bacon grease from the pan, then add remaining ingredients and mix by using an electric hand mixer until combined.
- Shape the mixture into balls, roll each ball into chopped bacon until coated, and then serve.

Dinner – Chicken and Cabbage Plate

Serving: 2
Preparation time: 10 minutes; Cooking time: 10 minutes;
Nutritional Info: 261 Cal; 23 g Fats; 12 g Protein; 1.75 g Net Carb; 0.7 g Fiber;
Ingredients
- 2 chicken thighs, pasteurized
- 4 ounces green cabbage, shredded
- 2 scallions, sliced
- 2 tablespoons coconut oil
- 1/4 cup mayonnaise

Extra:
- 1/2 teaspoon salt
- 1/2 teaspoon ground black pepper

Directions
- Take a frying pan, place it over medium heat, add 1 tablespoon oil and wait until it melts.
- Season chicken with ¼ teaspoon salt and black pepper, add to the frying pan, and cook for 5 minutes per side until thoroughly cooked.
- When done, transfer chicken to a cutting board, let it cool for 5 minutes, and then shred by using two forks.
- Distribute cabbage and scallion between two plates, top with shredded chicken and mayonnaise, drizzle with remaining oil and season with remaining salt and black pepper.
- Serve straight away.

Day 61

Breakfast – Coconut Porridge

Serving: 2
Preparation time: 5 minutes; Cooking time: 0 minutes;
Nutritional Info: 243 Cal; 24 g Fats; 4.5 g Protein; 2 g Net Carb; 2.5 g Fiber;
Ingredients
- 2 tablespoons coconut flour
- ¼ teaspoon ground psyllium husk powder
- 2 eggs, beaten
- 3 ounces coconut cream, full-fat
- 2 ounces of coconut oil

Extra:
- 1/8 teaspoon salt

Directions
- Take a medium bowl, crack eggs in it, then add flour, salt, and husk powder and whisk until combined.
- Take a small heatproof bowl, add butter and cream in it, and then microwave for 30 to 45 seconds at high heat setting until melts.
- Slowly stir melted butter-cream mixture into the flour until creamy and then distribute between two bowls.
- Top porridge with nuts and then serve.

Lunch – Meat and Feta Cheese Plate

Serving: 2
Preparation time: 5 minutes; Cooking time: 10 minutes;
Nutritional Info: 536 Cal; 47 g Fats; 25 g Protein; 1.9 g Net Carb; 0.8 g Fiber;
Ingredients
- 2 chicken thighs, pasteurized
- 2 ounces feta cheese, full-fat
- ½ cup shredded cabbage
- 8 green olives
- 1/3 cup olive oil

Extra:
- 1/2 teaspoon salt
- 1/2 teaspoon ground black pepper

Directions
- Take a frying pan, place it over medium heat, add 1 tablespoon oil and wait until it melts.
- Season chicken with ¼ teaspoon salt and black pepper, add to the frying pan, and cook for 5 minutes per side until thoroughly cooked.
- While the chicken cooked, shred the cabbage and then cut feta cheese into cubes.
- Distribute chicken between two plates, add cabbage, olives and feta cheese and then season with remaining salt and black pepper.
- Serve with remaining olive oil.

Dinner – Tuna and Avocado

Serving: 2
Preparation time: 5 minutes; Cooking time: 0 minutes;
Nutritional Info: 680 Cal; 65.6 g Fats; 10.2 g Protein; 2.2 g Net Carb; 9.7 g Fiber;
Ingredients
- 2 ounces tuna, packed in water
- 1 avocado, pitted
- 8 green olives
- ½ cup mayonnaise, full-fat

Extra:
- 1/3 teaspoon salt
- 1/4 teaspoon ground black pepper

Directions

- Cut avocado into half, then remove the pit, scoop out the flesh and distribute between two plates.
- Add tuna and green olives and then season with salt and black pepper.
- Serve with mayonnaise.

Day 62

Breakfast – Cheese Roll-Ups

Serving: 2
Preparation time: 5 minutes; Cooking time: 0 minutes;
Nutritional Info: 166 Cal; 15 g Fats; 6.5 g Protein; 2 g Net Carb; 0 g Fiber;
Ingredients

- 2 ounces mozzarella cheese, sliced, full-fat
- 1-ounce butter, unsalted

Directions

- Cut cheese into slices and then cut butter into thin slices.
- Top each cheese slice with a slice of butter, roll it and then serve.

Lunch – Salad Sandwiches

Serving: 2
Preparation time: 5 minutes; Cooking time: 0 minutes;
Nutritional Info: 187 Cal; 42.5 g Fats; 5 g Protein; 1.5 g Net Carb; 4 g Fiber;
Ingredients

- 2 cabbage leaves
- 1 avocado, pitted
- 1-ounce butter, unsalted
- 2 ounces feta cheese, sliced, full-fat

Directions

- Divide cabbage leaves into two parts, then smear them with butter and top with cheese.
- Cut avocado in half, remove the pit, scoop out the flesh and then top it onto each cabbage.
- Roll the cabbage and then serve straight away.

Dinner – Grilled Curry Chicken

Serving: 2
Preparation time: 35 minutes; Cooking time: 10 minutes;
Nutritional Info: 221 Cal; 12.8 g Fats; 25 g Protein; 1.7 g Net Carb; 0 g Fiber;
Ingredients

- 2 chicken thighs, pasteurized
- 2/3 tablespoon curry powder
- 1 tablespoon coconut oil
- 6 tablespoons Greek yogurt, full-fat

Extra:

- 1/4 teaspoon salt
- 1/4 teaspoon ground black pepper

Directions

- Take a medium bowl, add yogurt in it, and then whisk in salt, black pepper,

and curry powder.
- Add chicken thighs, toss until well coated and let it marinate in the refrigerator for 30 minutes.

- When ready to cook, take a griddle pan, place it over medium-high heat, grease it with oil and when hot, add marinated

chicken and cook for 5 minutes per side until thoroughly cooked.
- Serve straight away.

Day 63
Breakfast – Tuna Egg Boats

Serving: 2
Preparation time: 5 minutes; Cooking time: 12 minutes;
Nutritional Info: 224 Cal; 15.4 g Fats; 15.7 g Protein; 1 g Net Carb; 9.2 g Fiber;
Ingredients
- 2 ounces tuna, packed in water
- 1 avocado, pitted
- 2 eggs, pasteurized

Extra:
- ¼ teaspoon salt
- 1/8 teaspoon ground black pepper

Directions
- Switch on the oven, then set it to 425 degrees F and let it preheat.
- Meanwhile, prepare the avocado and for this, cut the avocado into half,

remove the pit and then scoop out some of the flesh to make the hollow bigger.
- Distribute tuna evenly between avocado halves, crack the egg into each hollow and bake the egg boats for 10 to 12 minutes until the egg has cooked to the desired level.
- When done, season egg boats with salt and black pepper and serve.

Lunch – Garlic Butter Zucchini Noodles

Serving: 2
Preparation time: 5 minutes; Cooking time: 5 minutes;
Nutritional Info: 287 Cal; 25.5 g Fats; 2.9 g Protein; 7.6 g Net Carb; 3.9 g Fiber;
Ingredients

- 2 medium zucchini
- 2 teaspoons dried cilantro
- ½ of a lime, juiced
- 2 tablespoons butter, unsalted
- 2 tablespoons olive oil

Extra:
- 2/3 tablespoon Sriracha sauce
- 1/3 teaspoon red chili flakes
- ¼ teaspoon salt
- ¼ teaspoon ground black pepper

Directions
- Prepare zucchini noodles and for this, trim the ends of zucchini and then spiralize them by using a vegetable peeler or a spiralizer.
- Take a medium skillet pan, place it over medium heat, add butter and oil and when the butter melts, add 1 teaspoon cilantro, lime juice, Sriracha sauce, and red pepper flakes,

stir until mixed and cook for 1 minute until fragrant.

- Add zucchini noodles, toss until coated, and then cook for 3 minutes until tender-crisp.
- Season with salt and black pepper, then distribute zucchini between two plates, top with remaining cilantro and then serve.

Dinner – Cabbage with Crispy Bacon

Serving: 2
Preparation time: 5 minutes; Cooking time: 10 minutes;
Nutritional Info: 425 Cal; 39 g Fats; 10 g Protein; 4.5 g Net Carb; 3 g Fiber;
Ingredients

- 4 ounces green cabbage, chopped
- 4 slices of bacon, pasteurized
- 2 ounces butter, unsalted

Extra:

- 1/3 teaspoon salt
- 1/4 teaspoon ground black pepper

Directions

- Take a medium skillet pan, place it over medium heat and when hot, add bacon and cook for 3 minutes per side until crisps.
- Transfer bacon to a cutting board, let it cool for 5 minutes and then chop it.
- Add butter to the pan and when it melts, add cabbage, toss until mixed and fry for 4 to 5 minutes until golden brown and softened.
- Season cabbage with salt and black pepper, return bacon into the pan, stir until mixed and remove the pan from heat.
- Distribute cabbage and bacon between two plates and then serve.

Week 10

Shopping List for Week 10

Remaining foods from the previous week(s):
- 1 ounce chopped lettuce
- 10 oz. coconut flour
- 1 oz. tuna, packed in water
- 4 oz. spinach leaves
- 2 ounces whipped cream
- 3 eggs
- 1 oz. feta cheese
- 2 oz. green olives
- Scallion
- 8 oz. coconut cream

Look in pantry for:
- Himalayan pink salt/sea salt
- Organic black pepper
- Organic Red pepper flakes

- Organic Red chili powder
- Organic Paprika
- Garlic
- Dried parsley
- Oregano
- Liquid stevia
- Coconut sugar
- Baking powder
- Psyllium husk
- Almonds
- Thai red curry paste
- White wine vinegar
- Avocado oil
- Coconut oil
- Butter
- Teabag
- Mayonnaise
- Greek yogurt

Purchase the following:

Items:	Store:	Quantity:	Price:
Large White Eggs, 12 count, 24 oz.	Walmart	1	1.38
Mozzarella cheese, 8 oz.	Walmart	1	1.54
Hass avocado	Walmart	2	0.8
Roma tomato	Walmart	2	0.27
Wild-caught Mahi-Mahi fillets, 12 oz., 4 count	Walmart	1	5.1
Wild-caught pacific whitening fillet, skin on 2 lb., count 10	Walmart	1	5.1
Sliced roast beef, 7 oz.	Walmart	1	1.78
Frozen broccoli and cauliflower 12 oz.	Walmart	1	0.75
Kale bunch	Walmart	1	0.6
Brussels sprouts 12 oz.	Walmart	1	1.1
Turkey Bacon 6 oz.	Walmart	1	1.12
Lime, count 1	Walmart	1	0.25
		Total:	19.79

Day 64

Breakfast – Cheesy Garlic Chaffles

Serving: 2
Preparation time: 5 minutes; Cooking time: 10 minutes;
Nutritional Info: 208 Cal; 16 g Fats; 11 g Protein; 2 g Net Carb; 2 g Fiber;
Ingredients
1. 1/4 teaspoon baking powder
2. ½ teaspoon minced garlic
3. 1 pasteurized egg
4. 2/3 cup shredded mozzarella cheese, full-fat

Extra:
5. 1/2 teaspoon Italian seasoning

Directions
- Switch on a mini waffle maker and let it preheat for 5 minutes.
- Meanwhile, take a medium bowl, place all the ingredients in it and then mix by using an immersion blender until smooth.
- Ladle the batter evenly into the waffle maker, shut with lid, and let it cook for 3 to 4 minutes until firm and golden brown.
- Serve straight away.

Lunch – Red Curry Glazed Mahi-Mahi

Serving: 2
Preparation time: 5 minutes; Cooking time: 7 minutes;
Nutritional Info: 272 Cal; 14 g Fats; 32 g Protein; 2 g Net Carb; 0 g Fiber;
Ingredients
1. 2 wild-caught Mahi-Mahi fillets
2. 1/2 tablespoon Thai red curry paste
3. 1/2 teaspoon coconut sugar
4. 1 tablespoon coconut oil

Extra:
5. ¼ teaspoon salt
6. ¼ teaspoon ground black pepper

Directions
- Switch on the broiler and let it preheat.
- Take a baking sheet, line it with aluminum foil, and then place salmon on it.
- Take a small bowl, add salt, black pepper, sugar, red curry paste and oil and stir until well combined.
- Brush the paste on all sides of fish and then broil for 7 minutes until cooked through and glazed.
- Serve straight away.

Dinner –Roast Beef and Vegetable Plate

Serving: 2
Preparation time: 10 minutes; Cooking time: 10 minutes;
Nutritional Info: 313 Cal; 26 g Fats; 15.6 g Protein; 2.8 g Net Carb; 1.9 g Fiber;
Ingredients
1. 2 scallions, chopped in large pieces
2. 1 ½ tablespoon coconut oil
3. 4 thin slices of roast beef
4. 4 ounces cauliflower and broccoli mix
5. 1 tablespoon butter, unsalted

Extra:
6. 1/2 teaspoon salt
7. 1/3 teaspoon ground black pepper
8. 1 teaspoon dried parsley

Directions
- Switch on the oven, then set it to 400 degrees F, and let it preheat.

- Take a baking sheet, grease it with oil, place slices of roast beef on one side, and top with butter.
- Take a separate bowl, add cauliflower and broccoli mix, add scallions, drizzle

with oil, season with remaining salt and black pepper, toss until coated and then spread vegetables on the empty side of the baking sheet.
- Bake for 5 to 7 minutes until beef is nicely

browned and vegetables are tender-crisp, tossing halfway.
- Distribute beef and vegetables between two plates and then serve.

Day 65
Breakfast – Ice Tea

Serving: 2
Preparation time: 2 hours and 5 minutes; Cooking time: 0 minutes;
Nutritional Info: 0 Cal; 0 g Fats; 0 g Protein; 0 g Net Carb; 0 g Fiber;
Ingredients
  1. 1 teabag
  2. 2 cups cold water
  3. 1 cup of ice cubes
Directions
- Take a pitcher, pour in 1 cup water, add the teabag and let it steep for 2 hours in the refrigerator.
- Then remove and discard tea bag, pour in remaining water, add ice cubes, and serve.

Lunch – Roast Beef and Mozzarella Plate

Serving: 2
Preparation time: 5 minutes; Cooking time: 0 minutes;
Nutritional Info: 267.7 Cal; 24.5 g Fats; 9.5 g Protein; 1.5 g Net Carb; 2 g Fiber;
Ingredients
  1. 4 slices of roast beef
  2. ½ ounce chopped lettuce
  3. 1 avocado, pitted
  4. 2 ounces mozzarella cheese, cubed
  5. ½ cup mayonnaise
Extra:
  6. ¼ teaspoon salt
  7. 1/8 teaspoon ground black pepper

  8. 2 tablespoons avocado oil
Directions
- Scoop out flesh from avocado and divide it evenly between two plates.
- Add slices of roast beef, lettuce, and cheese and then sprinkle with salt and black pepper.
- Serve with avocado oil and mayonnaise.

Dinner – Baked Fish with Feta and Tomato

Serving: 2
Preparation time: 5 minutes; Cooking time: 15 minutes;
Nutritional Info: 427.5 Cal; 29.5 g Fats; 26.7 g

Protein; 8 g Net Carb; 4 g Fiber;

Ingredients

1. 2 wild-caught pacific whitening fillets
2. 1 scallion, chopped
3. 1 Roma tomato, chopped
4. 1 teaspoon fresh oregano
5. 1-ounce feta cheese, crumbled

Extra:

6. 2 tablespoons avocado oil
7. 1/3 teaspoon salt
8. 1/4 teaspoon ground black pepper

9. ¼ crushed red pepper

Directions

- Switch on the oven, then set it to 400 degrees F and let it preheat.
- Take a medium skillet pan, place it over medium heat, add oil and when hot, add scallion and cook for 3 minutes.
- Add tomatoes, stir in ½ teaspoon oregano, 1/8 teaspoon salt, black pepper, red

pepper, pour in ¼ cup water and bring it to simmer.

- Sprinkle remaining salt over fillets, add to the pan, drizzle with remaining oil, and then bake for 10 to 12 minutes until fillets are fork-tender.
- When done, top fish with remaining oregano and cheese and then serve.

Day 66

Breakfast – Broccoll and Mozzarella Muffins

Serving: 2
Preparation time: 5 minutes; Cooking time: 12 minutes;
Nutritional Info: 135 Cal; 9.5 g Fats; 9.1 g Protein; 1.4 g Net Carb; 0.6 g Fiber;
Ingredients

10. 1/3 cup chopped broccoli
11. 2 pasteurized eggs
12. 1 tablespoon coconut cream
13. 2 tablespoons grated

mozzarella cheese, full-fat

Extra:

14. ¼ teaspoon salt
15. ¼ teaspoon ground black pepper

Directions

- Switch on the oven, then set it to 350 degrees F and let it preheat.
- Take a medium bowl, crack eggs in it and whisk in salt, black pepper, and cream until well combined.
- Add broccoli and cheese, stir until mixed, divide the batter evenly between two silicone muffin

cups, and bake for 10 to 12 minutes until firm and the top has golden brown.

- When done, let muffin cool for 5 minutes, then take them out and serve.

Lunch – Sprouts and Kale Sauté

Serving: 2
Preparation time: 5 minutes; Cooking time: 5 minutes;
Nutritional Info: 210 Cal; 17.5 g Fats; 4.7 g

Protein; 1.9 g Net Carb; 6 g Fiber;

Ingredients

1. 2 ounces chopped kale
2. 4 ounces Brussels sprouts
3. 3 tablespoons chopped almonds
4. 1 tablespoon white wine vinegar
5. 1 ½ tablespoon avocado oil

Extra:

6. 1/3 teaspoon salt

Directions

- Prepare the sprout and for this, peel the leaves, starting from outside and continue peeling towards to middle until you reach the tough core.
- Discard the core and transfer sprout leaves to a medium bowl.
- Take a large frying pan, place it over medium heat, add oil and when hot, add sprout leaves, toss until coated with oil, and cook for 1 minute or until sauté.

- Drizzle with vinegar, add kale, toss until mixed, and cook for 1 minute until kale leaves begin to wilt.
- Season with salt, remove the pan from heat and garnish with almonds.
- Serve straight away.

Dinner – Garlic Oregano Fish

Serving: 2
Preparation time: 5 minutes; Cooking time: 12 minutes;
Nutritional Info: 199.5 Cal; 7 g Fats; 33.5 g Protein; 0.9 g Net Carb; 0.1 g Fiber;

Ingredients

1. 2 wild-caught pacific whitening fillets
2. 1 teaspoon minced garlic
3. 1 tablespoon butter, unsalted

4. 2 teaspoons dried oregano

Extra:

5. 1/3 teaspoon salt
6. 1/4 teaspoon ground black pepper

Directions

- Switch on the oven, then set it to 400 degrees F and let it preheat.
- Meanwhile, take a small saucepan, place it over low heat, add butter and when it melts, stir in garlic and cook for 1 minute, remove the pan from heat.
- Season fillets with salt and black pepper, and place them on a baking dish greased with oil.
- Pour butter mixture over fillets, then sprinkle with oregano and bake for 10 to 12 minutes until thoroughly cooked.
- Serve straight away.

Day 67

Breakfast – Bacon and Cheese Roll-ups

Serving: 2
Preparation time: 10 minutes; Cooking time: 10 minutes;
Nutritional Info: 165 Cal; 12.5 g Fats; 12.4 g Protein; 0.8 g Net Carb; 0 g Fiber;
Ingredients

1. 2 ounces mozzarella cheese, sliced, full-fat
2. 4 slices of bacon

Directions

- Take a skillet pan, place it over medium heat and when hot, add bacon slices and cook for 3 minutes per side until crisp.
- When done, transfer bacon to the cutting board, cool for 5 minutes, and then chop.
- Cut cheese into thin slices, top with chopped bacon, and then roll the cheese.
- Serve straight away.

Lunch – Sprouts and Bacon Plate

Serving: 2
Preparation time: 5 minutes; Cooking time: 8 minutes;
Nutritional Info: 145 Cal; 11.2 g Fats; 5.4 g Protein; 3.2 g Net Carb; 2.2 g Fiber;
Ingredients

1. 4 ounces Brussels sprouts
2. 1 teaspoon minced garlic
3. 3 slices of bacon, chopped
4. 1 teaspoon avocado oil

Extra:

5. 1/3 teaspoon salt
6. 1/4 teaspoon ground black pepper

Directions

- Take a medium skillet pan, place it over medium heat and when hot, add bacon and cook for 3 minutes per side until crisp.
- Add sprouts, add oil, toss until mixed and cook for 10 minutes until thoroughly cooked.
- Stir in garlic, season with salt and black pepper and continue cooking for 1 minute.
- Serve straight away.

Dinner – Fish and Spinach Plate

Serving: 2
Preparation time: 10 minutes; Cooking time: 10 minutes;
Nutritional Info: 389 Cal; 34 g Fats; 7.7 g Protein; 10.6 g Net Carb; 2 g Fiber;
Ingredients

10. 2 wild-caught pacific whitening fillets
11. 2 ounces spinach
12. ½ cup mayonnaise
13. 1 tablespoon avocado oil
14. 1 tablespoon unsalted butter

Extra:

15. 1/2 teaspoon salt
16. 1/3 teaspoon ground black pepper

Directions

- Take a frying pan, place it over medium heat, add butter and wait until it melts.
- Season fillets with 1/3 teaspoon salt and ¼ teaspoon black pepper, add to the pan, and cook for 5 minutes per side until golden

brown and thoroughly cooked.
- Transfer fillets to two plates, then

distribute spinach among them, drizzle with oil and season with remaining salt

and black pepper.
- Serve with mayonnaise.

Day 68

Breakfast – Scrambled Eggs with Spinach and Cheese

Serving: 2
Preparation time: 5 minutes; Cooking time: 5 minutes;
Nutritional Info: 171 Cal; 14 g Fats; 9.2 g Protein; 1.1 g Net Carb; 1.7 g Fiber;
Ingredients
1. 2 ounces spinach
2. 2 pasteurized eggs
3. 1 tablespoon coconut oil
4. 2 tablespoons grated mozzarella cheese, full-fat

Extra:
5. ¼ teaspoon salt
6. 1/8 teaspoon ground black pepper
7. 1/8 teaspoon red pepper flakes

Directions
- Take a medium bowl, crack eggs in it, add salt and black pepper and

whisk until combined.
- Take a medium skillet pan, place it over medium heat, add oil and when hot, add spinach and cook for 1 minute until leaves wilt.
- Pour eggs over spinach, stir and cook for 1 minute until just set.
- Stir in cheese, then remove the pan from heat and sprinkle red pepper flakes on top.
- Serve straight away.

Lunch – Salad in Jar

Serving: 2
Preparation time: 5 minutes; Cooking time: 0 minutes;
Nutritional Info: 438 Cal; 38 g Fats; 13.5 g Protein; 5.5 g Net Carb; 8.5 g Fiber;
Ingredients

1. 2 ounces chopped kale
2. 1 scallion, chopped
3. 1 avocado, pitted, chopped
4. 1 Roma tomato, chopped
5. 4 slices of beef roast, diced

Extra:
6. ½ cup mayonnaise

Directions
- Take two mason jars, place kale evenly at the bottom and then top with kale, scallion, avocado, and tomato.
- Top with beef and serve each jar with ¼ cup mayonnaise.

Dinner – Fish with Kale and Olives

Serving: 2
Preparation time: 5 minutes; Cooking time: 12 minutes;

Nutritional Info: 454 Cal; 35.8 g Fats; 16 g Protein; 13.5 g Net Carb; 3.5 g Fiber;

Ingredients

1. 2 wild-caught pacific whitening fillets
2. 2 ounces chopped kale
3. 3 tablespoons coconut oil
4. 2 scallion, chopped
5. 6 green olives

Extra:

6. 1/2 teaspoon salt
7. 1/3 teaspoon ground black pepper
8. 3 drops of liquid stevia

Directions

- Take a large skillet pan, place it over medium-high heat, add 4 tablespoons water, then add kale, toss and cook for 2 minutes until leaves are wilted but green.
- When done, transfer kale to a strainer placed on a bowl and set aside until required.
- Wipe clean the pan, add 2 tablespoons oil, and wait until it melts.
- Season fillets with 1/3 teaspoon salt and ¼ teaspoon black pepper, place them into the pan skin-side up and cook for 4 minutes per side until fork tender.
- Transfer fillets to a plate, add remaining oil to the pan, then add scallion and olives and cook for 1 minute.
- Return kale into the pan, stir until mixed, cook for 1 minute until hot and then season with remaining salt and black pepper.
- Divide kale mixture between two plates, top with cooked fillets, and then serve.

Day 69

Breakfast – Yogurt Chaffles

Serving: 2
Preparation time: 5 minutes; Cooking time: 4 minutes;
Nutritional Info: 100 Cal; 100 g Fats; 100 g Protein; 100 g Net Carb; 100 g Fiber;

Ingredients

1. 2 tablespoons coconut flour
2. ½ teaspoon Psyllium husk
3. 1 pasteurized egg
4. 1/3 cup shredded mozzarella cheese, full-fat
5. 1 tablespoon Greek yogurt, full-fat

Extra:

6. ¼ teaspoon baking powder

Directions

- Switch on a mini waffle maker and let it preheat for 5 minutes.
- Meanwhile, take a medium bowl, crack eggs in it and whisk by using a fork until blended.
- Then add remaining ingredients except for cheese, stir until smooth batter comes together, stir in cheese and let the batter stand for 3 minutes.
- Ladle the batter evenly into the waffle maker,

shut with lid, and let it cook for 3 to 4 minutes until firm and golden brown.

- Serve straight away.

Lunch – Beef and Broccoli

Serving: 2
Preparation time: 5 minutes; Cooking time: 10 minutes;
Nutritional Info: 245 Cal; 15.7 g Fats; 21.6 g Protein; 1.7 g Net Carb; 1.3 g Fiber;
Ingredients
1. 6 slices of beef roast, cut into strips
2. 1 scallion, chopped
3. 3 ounces broccoli florets, chopped
4. 1 tablespoon avocado oil
5. 1 tablespoon butter, unsalted

Extra:
6. ¼ teaspoon salt
7. 1/8 teaspoon ground black pepper
8. 1 ½ tablespoon soy sauce
9. 3 tablespoons chicken broth

Directions
- Take a medium skillet pan, place it over medium heat, add oil and when hot, add beef strips and cook for 2 minutes until hot.
- Transfer beef to a plate, add scallion to the pan, then add butter and cook for 3 minutes until tender.
- Add remaining ingredients, stir until mixed, switch heat to the low level and simmer for 3 to 4 minutes until broccoli is tender.
- Return beef to the pan, stir until well combined and cook for 1 minute.
- Serve straight away.

Dinner – Baked Sprouts Casserole

Serving: 2
Preparation time: 10 minutes; Cooking time: 25 minutes;
Nutritional Info: 235 Cal; 19.7 g Fats; 9.3 g Protein; 3.1 g Net Carb; 1.6 g Fiber;
Ingredients
1. 2 slices of bacon, cooked, crumbled
2. 2 ounces Brussels sprouts, halved
3. 3 tablespoons coconut cream
4. ½ of egg
5. 4 tablespoons grated mozzarella cheese, full-fat

Extra:
6. ¼ teaspoon salt
7. 1/8 teaspoon ground black pepper
8. ¼ teaspoon paprika
9. ¾ tablespoon avocado oil

Directions
- Switch on the oven, then set it to 400 degrees F and let it preheat.
- Take a medium bowl, add sprouts in it, drizzle with oil, season with salt and black pepper and toss until well coated.
- Spread sprouts into a casserole dish and then bake for 15 minutes until tender.
- Meanwhile, take a separate medium bowl, crack the egg in it, add cheese cream, paprika and whisk until well combined.
- When sprouts have cooked, top them with crumbled bacon, let the mixture cool for 5 minutes, then top with egg mixture and bake for 7 to 10 minutes until the top has

turned nicely   browned.

Day 70

Breakfast – Cheese Omelet

Serving: 2
Preparation time: 5 minutes; Cooking time: 10 minutes;
Nutritional Info: 275 Cal; 25.7 g Fats; 10.3 g Protein; 0.7 g Net Carb; 0 g Fiber;
Ingredients
1. 1.5 ounces butter, unsalted
2. 2 pasteurized eggs
3. 1 ounce shredded mozzarella cheese, full-fat

Extra:
4. ¼ teaspoon salt
5. 1/8 teaspoon ground black pepper

Directions
- Take a medium bowl, crack eggs in it, whisk until blended and then whisk in half of the cheese, salt, and black pepper.
- Take a frying pan, place it over medium heat, add butter and when it melts, pour in egg mixture, spread it evenly and let it cook for 2 minutes until set.
- Switch heat to the low level, continue cooking for 2 minutes until thoroughly cooked, and then top with remaining cheese.
- Fold the omelet, slide it to a plate, cut it in half, and then serve.

Lunch – Fish and Egg Plate

Serving: 2
Preparation time: 5 minutes; Cooking time: 10 minutes;
Nutritional Info: 547 Cal; 44.4 g Fats; 19.1 g Protein; 11.8 g Net Carb; 12 g Fiber;
Ingredients
1. 2 pasteurized eggs
2. 1 tablespoon butter, unsalted
3. 2 wild-caught pacific whitening fillets
4. ½ ounces chopped lettuce
5. 1 scallion, chopped

Extra:
6. 3 tablespoons avocado oil
7. 1/3 teaspoon salt
8. 1/3 teaspoon ground black pepper

Directions
- Cook the eggs and for this, take a frying pan, place it over medium heat, add butter and when it melts, crack the egg in the pan and cook for 2 to 3 minutes until fried to desired liking.
- Transfer fried egg to a plate and then cook the remaining egg in the same manner.
- Meanwhile, season fish fillets with ¼ teaspoon each of salt and black pepper.
- When eggs have fried, sprinkle salt and black pepper on them, then add 1 tablespoon oil into the frying pan, add fillets and cook for 4 minutes per side

until thoroughly cooked.

- When done, distribute fillets to the plate, add lettuce and scallion, drizzle with remaining oil, and then serve.

Dinner – Mahi-Mahi with Chili Lime Butter

Serving: 2
Preparation time: 5 minutes; Cooking time: 10 minutes;
Nutritional Info: 298 Cal; 18.2 g Fats; 31.5 g Protein; 0.1 g Net Carb; 0.2 g Fiber;

Ingredients

1. 3 tablespoons coconut oil, divided
2. ½ teaspoon red chili powder
3. 2 mahi-mahi fillets
4. 1 lime, zested

Extra:

5. 1/3 teaspoon salt
6. ¼ teaspoon ground black pepper

Directions

- Prepare the chili-lime butter and for this, take a small bowl, add 2 tablespoons coconut oil in it and then stir in red chili powder and lime zest until combined, set aside until required.
- Take a medium skillet pan, place it over medium-high heat, add remaining oil and wait until it melts.
- Season fillets with salt and black pepper, add to the pan and cook for 5 minutes per side until thoroughly cooked and golden brown.
- When done, transfer fillets to the plates, top generously with prepared chili-lime butter, and then serve.

Week 11
<u>Shopping List for Week 11</u>

Remaining foods from the previous week(s):
- 9 oz. coconut flour
- 1 oz. tuna, packed in water
- 2 ounces whipped cream
- 6 oz. coconut cream
- 8 oz. frozen broccoli and cauliflower
- 2 oz. kale
- 2 oz. Brussels Sprouts
- 2 oz. turkey bacon

Look in pantry for:
- Himalayan pink salt/sea salt
- Organic black pepper
- Erythritol sweetener
- Organic onion powder
- Organic garlic powder
- Organic ginger powder
- Tex-mex seasoning
- All-purpose seasoning
- Chipotle seasoning

- Italian seasoning
- Greek seasoning
- Curry powder
- Red pepper flakes
- Organic cinnamon
- Organic ground cumin
- Organic dried thyme
- Organic dried rosemary
- Baking powder
- Sesame seeds
- Almonds
- Oregano
- Coffee powder
- Chili-garlic paste
- Soy sauce
- Hot sauce
- Avocado oil
- Coconut oil
- MCT oil
- Sesame oil
- Butter
- Mayonnaise
- Hot BBQ sauce, keto

Purchase the following:

Items:	Store:	Quantity:	Price:
Large White Eggs, 12 count, 24 oz.	Walmart	1	1.38
Tuna in water, 5 oz.	Walmart	1	0.76
Thin sliced roast beef, 7 oz.	Walmart	1	1.6
Brussel Sprouts 12 oz.	Walmart	1	1.1
Lime count 1	Walmart	1	0.25
Shredded parmesan cheese, 10 oz.	Walmart	1	1.4
Spinach 10 oz.	Walmart	1	1.1
Broccoli and cauliflower 12 oz.	Walmart	1	1
Coconut milk 14 oz.	Walmart	1	1.4
Ground flaxseed 8 oz.	Walmart	1	1.2
Ground turkey 16 oz.	Walmart	1	2.8
Boneless skinless chicken thighs 2.5 pound 6 to 8 count	Walmart	1	5.2
Lettuce leaf	Walmart	1	1.2
		Total:	19.85

Day 71

Breakfast – Coconut Coffee

Serving: 2
Preparation time: 5 minutes; Cooking time: 0 minutes;
Nutritional Info: 230 Cal; 25 g Fats; 0 g Protein; 0 g Net Carb; 0 g Fiber;
Ingredients
- 2 cups brewed coffee
- ½ teaspoon ground cinnamon
- 2 tablespoons coconut oil

Directions
1. Pour coffee into a blender or food processor, add oil and butter and then blend for 10 seconds until light and creamy.
2. Distribute coffee among two mugs, sprinkle with cinnamon and then serve.

Lunch – Burger Plate

Serving: 2
Preparation time: 10 minutes; Cooking time: 10 minutes;
Nutritional Info: 283 Cal; 24.6 g Fats; 12 g Protein; 2 g Net Carb; 2.6 g Fiber;
Ingredients
- 3 ounces ground turkey
- 1 tablespoon tex-mex seasoning
- 2 tablespoons avocado oil
- 2 ounces chopped lettuce
- 1/3 cup mayonnaise

Extra:
- ¼ teaspoon salt
- ¼ teaspoon ground black pepper

Directions
1. Take a medium bowl, place ground turkey in it, add tex-mex seasoning, salt, and black pepper, stir until well combined, and shape the mixture into two patties.
2. Take a medium skillet pan, place it over medium heat, add oil and when hot, add prepared patties and cook for 4 minutes per side until golden brown and thoroughly cooked.
3. When done, distribute patties between two plates, add lettuce, and serve with mayonnaise.

Dinner – Garlic and Buttery Brussel Sprouts with Bacon

Serving: 2
Preparation time: 5 minutes; Cooking time: 18 minutes;
Nutritional Info: 312 Cal; 12 g Fats; 11 g Protein; 4 g Net Carb; 4 g Fiber;
Ingredients
- 6 ounces Brussel sprouts, halved
- 1-ounce turkey bacon, chopped
- 1 tablespoon butter, unsalted
- 2 ½ tablespoons grated parmesan cheese
- 2 ounces coconut cream

Extra:
- ½ teaspoon garlic powder
- ¼ teaspoon salt
- 1/8 teaspoon ground black pepper

Directions
1. Switch on the oven, then set it to 375 degrees F and let it preheat.
2. Take a medium skillet pan, place it over medium heat and when hot, add chopped bacon and cook for 3 to 5 minutes until browned.

3. Transfer bacon to a plate lined with paper towels, drain most of the bacon fat from the skillet, then add butter and wait until it melts.
4. Add Brussel sprouts, toss until coated, season with salt

and black pepper and cook for 3 to 4 minutes until beginning to crisp.
5. Sprinkle with garlic, cook for 30 seconds until fragrant, then switch heat to the low level and pour cream over sprouts.

6. Simmer for 2 minutes, then sprinkle with bacon and cheese and bake for 5 to 7 minutes until cheese has melted and golden brown.
7. Serve straight away.

Day 72
Breakfast – Garlic Parmesan Chaffles

Serving: 2
Preparation time: 5 minutes; Cooking time: 10 minutes;
Nutritional Info: 208 Cal; 16 g Fats; 11 g Protein; 2 g Net Carb; 2 g Fiber;
Ingredients
- 1/4 teaspoon baking powder
- 1 teaspoon garlic powder
- 1 pasteurized egg
- 2/3 cup shredded parmesan cheese, full-fat

Extra:
- 1/2 teaspoon Italian seasoning

Directions
1. Switch on a mini waffle maker and let it preheat for 5 minutes.

2. Meanwhile, take a medium bowl, place all the ingredients in it and then mix by using an immersion blender until smooth.
3. Ladle the batter evenly into the waffle maker, shut with lid, and let it cook for 3 to 4 minutes until firm and golden brown.
Serve straight away.

Lunch – Lime Garlic Chicken Thighs

Serving: 2
Preparation time: 35 minutes; Cooking time: 15 minutes;

Nutritional Info: 260 Cal; 15.6 g Fats; 26.8 g Protein; 1.3 g Net Carb; 0.6 g Fiber;
Ingredients
- 2 boneless chicken thighs, pasteurized, skinless
- ¾ teaspoon garlic powder
- 1 ½ teaspoon all-purpose seasoning
- ½ of lime, juiced, zested
- 1 ½ tablespoon avocado oil

Directions
1. Take a medium bowl, place chicken in it, and sprinkle with garlic powder, all-purpose seasoning, and lime zest.
2. Drizzle with lime juice, toss until well coated and let chicken thighs marinate for 30 minutes.

3. Then take a medium skillet pan, place it over medium heat, add oil and when hot, place marinated chicken thighs in it and cook for 5 to 7 minutes per side until thoroughly cooked.
4. Serve straight away.

Dinner – Ground Turkey, Spinach and Eggs

Serving: 2
Preparation time: 5 minutes; Cooking time: 12 minutes;
Nutritional Info: 317 Cal; 21.5 g Fats; 27.5 g Protein; 1.5 g Net Carb; 1 g Fiber;

Ingredients
- 3 ounces ground turkey
- 2 ounces spinach
- 1 1/3 tablespoon butter, unsalted
- 2 eggs, pasteurized
- 1 tablespoon grated parmesan cheese

Extra:
- 2/3 teaspoon garlic powder
- 1 ½ teaspoon chipotle seasoning
- ½ teaspoon salt
- ¼ teaspoon ground black pepper

Directions
1. Take a medium skillet pan, place it over medium heat, add butter and when it melts, add turkey, sprinkle with garlic and cook for 3 to 5 minutes until nicely browned.
2. Add spinach, stir until mixed, and then cook for 2 to 3 minutes until spinach leaves wilts.
3. Crack eggs in a small bowl, whisk until frothy, add to the skillet pan, season with chipotle seasoning, salt, and black pepper and cook for 3 to 4 minutes until the egg has cooked.
4. Sprinkle with cheese, cook for 1 minute until cheese has melted and then serve.

Day 73

Breakfast – Cheesy Cauliflower Muffins

Serving: 2
Preparation time: 10 minutes; Cooking time: 12 minutes;
Nutritional Info: 77 Cal; 5.6 g Fats; 4.6 g Protein; 1.7 g Net Carb; 0.9 g Fiber;

Ingredients
- ¾ cup chopped cauliflower florets
- 1 egg, pasteurized
- 1 ¾ tablespoon coconut flour
- ¼ teaspoon Italian seasoning
- 1/3 cup grated parmesan cheese

Extra:
- ¼ teaspoon salt
- 1/8 teaspoon onion powder
- 1/8 teaspoon garlic powder

Directions
1. Switch on the oven, then set it to 375 degrees F and let it preheat.
2. Take a medium bowl, place chopped cauliflower in it, add flour, half of the cheese, onion powder, garlic powder, and Italian seasoning and stir until

incorporated and smooth.

3. Take four silicone cups, fill them with prepared cauliflower mixture, sprinkle remaining cheese on top and then bake for 10 to 12 minutes until thoroughly cooked and firm.

4. Serve straight away.

Lunch – Meatballs Lettuce Wrap

Serving: 2
Preparation time: 5 minutes; Cooking time: 10 minutes;
Nutritional Info: 412 Cal; 38 g Fats; 14.4 g Protein; 1.7 g Net Carb; 0.4 g Fiber;
Ingredients

- 3 ounces ground turkey
- ¼ teaspoon garlic powder
- 1/3 teaspoon ground cumin
- ¾ teaspoon Greek seasoning
- 2 lettuce leaves

Extra:

- 1/4 cup mayonnaise

- 1 tablespoon avocado oil

Directions

1. Take a medium bowl, place ground turkey in it, add garlic powder, cumin, and Greek seasoning, stir until well mixed and then shape the mixture into meatballs.

2. Take a medium skillet pan, place it over medium heat, add oil and when hot, add meatballs and cook for 2 to 3 minutes per side until golden brown and cooked.

3. Distribute meatballs between lettuce leaves, drizzle with mayonnaise, and then serve.

Dinner – Broccoli and Cauliflower in Cheese

Serving: 2
Preparation time: 5 minutes; Cooking time: 8 minutes;
Nutritional Info: 183.5 Cal; 15.5 g Fats; 7 g

Protein; 4.5 g Net Carb; 2.5 g Fiber;
Ingredients

- 4 ounces broccoli and cauliflower florets, medium chopped
- 2 tablespoons chopped oregano
- 3 tablespoons butter, unsalted
- 3 tablespoons grated parmesan cheese
- 1 ounce whipped cream

Extra:

- 1/3 teaspoon salt
- 1/4 teaspoon ground black pepper

Directions

1. Take a medium skillet pan, place it over medium-high heat, add butter and when it melts, add broccoli and cauliflower and cook for 3 to 4 minutes until golden brown.

2. Sprinkle with oregano, season with salt and black pepper, add cheese and cream, stir until well combined and cook for 1 to 2 minutes until cheese has melted.

3. Serve straight away.

Day 74

Breakfast – Coffee with Cinnamon

Serving: 2
Preparation time: 5 minutes; Cooking time: 10 minutes;
Nutritional Info: 140 Cal; 13.4 g Fats; 0.3 g Protein; 4 g Net Carb; 0.2 g Fiber;
Ingredients
- 2 cups brewed strong coffee
- 2 tablespoons MCT oil
- 1/3 teaspoon ground cinnamon

Directions
1. Distribute coffee among two cups, add 1 tablespoon of MCT oil into each cups, and then add cinnamon.
2. Stir until well combined and then serve.

Lunch – Garlic Herb Beef Roast

Serving: 2
Preparation time: 5 minutes; Cooking time: 10 minutes;
Nutritional Info: 140 Cal; 12.7 g Fats; 5.5 g Protein; 0.1 g Net Carb; 0.2 g Fiber;

Ingredients
- 6 slices of beef roast
- ½ teaspoon garlic powder
- 1/3 teaspoon dried thyme
- ¼ teaspoon dried rosemary
- 2 tablespoons butter, unsalted

Extra:
- 1/3 teaspoon salt
- 1/4 teaspoon ground black pepper

Directions
1. Prepare the spice mix and for this, take a small bowl, place garlic powder, thyme, rosemary, salt, and black pepper and then stir until mixed.
2. Sprinkle spice mix on the beef roast.
3. Take a medium skillet pan, place it over medium heat, add butter and when it melts, add beef roast and then cook for 5 to 8 minutes until golden brown and cooked.
4. Serve straight away.

Dinner – Chicken Coconut Curry

Serving: 2
Preparation time: 5 minutes; Cooking time: 15 minutes;
Nutritional Info: 177 Cal; 15.5 g Fats; 13.2 g Protein; 0.4 g Net Carb; 0.1 g Fiber;
Ingredients
- 2 boneless chicken thighs, pasteurized, skinless
- 2/3 teaspoon garlic powder
- 1 teaspoon curry powder
- ½ tablespoon avocado oil
- ½ cup coconut milk, unsweetened, full-fat

Extra:
- ½ teaspoon ginger powder
- 1/3 teaspoon salt
- ¼ teaspoon ground black pepper

Directions
1. Cut chicken into bite-size pieces and then season with salt and black pepper.
2. Take a medium saucepan, place it over medium heat, add oil and when hot, add chicken pieces and cook for 5 to 7 minutes until chicken is no longer pink and golden brown.
3. Take a medium bowl, pour coconut milk in

it, and then stir in curry powder.

4. Pour this mixture over chicken, bring it to simmer, then

switch heat to medium-low level and cook for 5 to 7 minutes or more until

chicken has cooked through.

5. Serve chicken curry with cauliflower rice.

Day 75

Breakfast – Egg Wrap with Bacon

Serving: 2
Preparation time: 10 minutes; Cooking time: 10 minutes;
Nutritional Info: 160 Cal; 10.7 g Fats; 12.8 g Protein; 1.9 g Net Carb; 0 g Fiber;
Ingredients
- 2 slices of turkey bacon, pasteurized
- 2 eggs, pasteurized
- 2 tablespoons grated parmesan cheese

Extra:
- 1/8 teaspoon salt
- 1/8 teaspoon ground black pepper

Directions
1. Take a medium bowl, crack eggs in it, add salt and black pepper, and then whisk until blended.
2. Take a medium skillet pan, place it over medium

heat and when hot, add bacon and cook for 3 to 5 minutes until crispy.
3. Transfer bacon to a cutting board, cool it for 3 minutes, chop it, and then set aside until required.
4. Pour half of the blended egg into the pan and then cook for 2 minutes or more until the egg has almost cooked.
5. Sprinkle 1 tablespoon of cheese on all over the egg, place half of the chopped bacon in the center of the roll, and then fold it on thirds.
6. Transfer egg roll to a plate and repeat with the remaining blended egg, bacon, and cheese.
7. Serve straight away.

Lunch – Sesame Tuna Salad

Serving: 2
Preparation time: 35 minutes; Cooking time: 0 minutes;
Nutritional Info: 322 Cal; 25.4 g Fats; 17.7 g Protein; 2.6 g Net Carb; 3 g Fiber;
Ingredients
- 6 ounces of tuna in water
- ½ tablespoon chili-garlic paste
- ½ tablespoon black sesame seeds, toasted
- 2 tablespoons mayonnaise
- 1 tablespoon sesame oil

Extra:
- 1/8 teaspoon red pepper flakes

Directions
1. Take a medium bowl, all the ingredients for the salad in it except for tuna, and then stir until well combined.

2. Fold in tuna until mixed and then refrigerator for 30 minutes.
3. Serve straight away.

Dinner – Teriyaki Turkey Rice Bowl

Serving: 2
Preparation time: 5 minutes; Cooking time: 15 minutes;
Nutritional Info: 210 Cal; 13.3 g Fats; 15 g Protein; 4.6 g Net Carb; 1.3 g Fiber;
Ingredients
- 3 ounces ground turkey

6. .

- 1 cup of broccoli rice
- ½ teaspoon sesame seeds
- 2 tablespoons avocado oil
- 3 tablespoons soy sauce

Extra:
- 1 teaspoon garlic powder
- 2/3 teaspoon salt
- ½ teaspoon red pepper flakes

Directions
1. Take a medium skillet pan, place it over medium heat, add 1 tablespoon oil and when hot, add broccoli rice and cook for 5 to 7 minutes until thoroughly cooked.
2. Remove pan from heat and then

distribute broccoli rice among two bowls.
3. Add remaining oil into the pan and when hot, add ground turkey and cook for 3 to 4 minutes until golden brown.
4. Sprinkle with garlic, salt, and red pepper flakes, drizzle with soy sauce, stir until mixed and cook for 4 to 5 minutes until thoroughly cooked.
5. Top ground turkey over broccoli, sprinkle with sesame seeds, and some red chili flakes and then serve

Day 76
Breakfast – Breakfast Flaxseed Pudding

Serving: 2
Preparation time: 35 minutes; Cooking time: 0 minutes;
Nutritional Info: 225 Cal; 17 g Fats; 6 g Protein; 1.6 g Net Carb; 8.8 g Fiber;
Ingredients

- ½ cup ground flaxseeds
- Pinch of salt
- 1 ½ tablespoon erythritol sweetener
- ¾ cup coconut milk, unsweetened, full-fat
- 2 tablespoons chopped almonds

Directions
1. Take a medium bowl, place flaxseeds in it, pour in the milk, and then stir in

salt and sweetener.
2. Let the pudding chill in the refrigerator for 30 minutes and then distribute between two bowls.
3. Top with almonds and favorite fruit slices and then serve.

Lunch – Brussel Leaf and Spinach Skillet

Serving: 2
Preparation time: 5 minutes; Cooking time: 10 minutes;
Nutritional Info: 235 Cal; 19.5 g Fats; 4.6 g Protein; 4.2 g Net Carb; 5 g Fiber;
Ingredients
- 4 ounce Brussels sprouts
- 4 ounces spinach
- ½ tablespoon erythritol sweetener
- 2 tablespoons avocado oil
- 3 tablespoons almonds, chopped

Extra:
- 1/3 teaspoon salt

Directions
1. Peel the leaves of the sprouts, starting from outside and continue peeling towards to middle until you reach the tough core, discard the core and transfer sprout leaves to a medium bowl.
2. Take a large frying pan, place it over medium heat, add oil and when hot, add sprout leaves, toss until coated with oil, and cook for 1 minute or until sauté.
3. Drizzle with vinegar, add spinach, toss until mixed, and cook for 1 minute until spinach leaves begin to wilt.
4. Season with salt, remove the pan from heat, and garnish with almonds.
5. Serve straight away.

Dinner – Ground Turkey with Cauliflower Skillet

Serving: 2
Preparation time: 5 minutes; Cooking time: 15 minutes;
Nutritional Info: 275 Cal; 21 g Fats; 12.6 g Protein; 5.4 g Net Carb; 1.2 g Fiber;
Ingredients
- 3 ounces ground turkey
- 4 ounces cauliflower florets, chopped
- ¼ of a lime, juiced
- 2 tablespoons avocado oil
- 3 tablespoons water

Extra:
- 2/3 teaspoon salt
- 1/2 teaspoon ground black pepper
- 1 ½ tablespoon soy sauce
- 1 tablespoon hot sauce

Directions
1. Take a medium skillet pan, place it over medium heat, add 1 tablespoon oil and when hot, add cauliflower florets and cook for 3 to 5 minutes until golden brown.
2. Drizzle lime juice over cauliflower florets, season with 1/3 teaspoon salt, ¼ teaspoon ground black pepper, stir until mixed and transfer cauliflower to a plate.
3. Return skillet pan over medium heat, add remaining oil and when hot, add turkey, crumble it and cook for 3 to 5 minutes until no longer pink.
4. Season with remaining salt and black pepper, drizzle with soy sauce and hot sauce, stir until mixed and cook for 3 minutes.
5. Push turkey to one side of the pan, add cauliflower florets to the empty side of the skillet, and cook for 2 minutes until florets are hot.

6. Serve straight away.

Day 77

Breakfast – Spinach Smoothie

Serving: 2
Preparation time: 5 minutes; Cooking time: 10 minutes;
Nutritional Info: 162 Cal; 15.2 g Fats; 1.2 g Protein; 2.2 g Net Carb; 1.7 g Fiber;
Ingredients
- 2 ounces spinach
- 1 ½ teaspoon ginger powder
- ¼ of lime, juiced
- 1/3 cup coconut milk, unsweetened, full-fat
- 2/3 cup water

Extra:
- 1 tablespoon avocado oil

Directions
1. Place all the ingredients in the order into a food processor or blender, and then pulse for 2 to 3 minutes until smooth.
2. Distribute smoothie among two glasses and then serve.

Lunch – Garlic Broccoli-Cauliflower Rice

Serving: 2
Preparation time: 5 minutes; Cooking time: 10 minutes;
Nutritional Info: 91 Cal; 8 g Fats; 3 g Protein; 6 g Net Carb; 2 g Fiber;
Ingredients
- 6 ounces broccoli and cauliflower, grated
- ½ teaspoon garlic powder
- 2 tablespoons butter, unsalted
- 2 tablespoons grated parmesan cheese
- 3 tablespoons water

Extra:
- 1/3 teaspoon salt
- 1/4 teaspoon ground black pepper

Directions
1. Take a medium heatproof bowl, place broccoli and cauliflower, and drizzle with water.
2. Cover with a plastic wrap, microwave for 2 minutes at high heat setting, then uncover the bowl and carefully drain the broccoli and cauliflower rice.
3. Take a frying pan, place it over medium heat, add butter and when it melts, add broccoli and cauliflower rice and cook for 2 to 3 minutes until beginning to brown.
4. Season with salt and black pepper, sprinkle with cheese and then serve.

Dinner – Cheesy BBQ Chicken Thighs

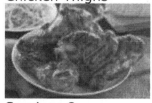

Serving: 2
Preparation time: 35 minutes; Cooking time: 10 minutes;
Nutritional Info: 293 Cal; 17.8 g Fats; 29.5 g Protein; 5 g Net Carb; 4 g Fiber;
Ingredients
- 2 boneless chicken thighs, pasteurized, skinless
- 1/3 teaspoon salt

- ¼ teaspoon ground black pepper
- 4 tablespoons hot BBQ sauce, keto
- 2 tablespoons grated parmesan cheese

Directions

1. Take a medium bowl, place chicken thighs in it, season with salt and black pepper, and then add BBQ sauce.
2. Toss until well coated and let it marinate in the refrigerator for 30 minutes.
3. Then take a griddle pan, place it over medium-high heat, grease it with oil and when hot, place chicken thighs on it, and then grill for 5 minutes per side until almost cooked, brushing with reserved BBQ marinade frequently.
4. Sprinkle with cheese, cook for 1 minute until cheese has melted and then serve.

Week 12

<u>Shopping List for Week 2</u>

Remaining foods from the previous week(s):

- 8 oz. coconut flour
- 2 oz. broccoli and cauliflower
- 1 oz. whipped cream
- 4 oz. coconut cream
- 2 oz. kale
- 4 oz. Brussels Sprouts
- 6 eggs
- 3.5 oz. sliced roast beef
- 2 oz. spinach
- 4 oz. flaxseed
- Lettuce leaf

Look in pantry for:

- Himalayan pink salt/sea salt
- Black pepper
- Organic onion powder
- Onion flakes
- Garlic powder
- Organic ginger powder
- Red pepper flakes
- Organic red chili powder
- Smoked paprika
- Organic dried rosemary
- Pumpkin pie spice
- Italian herb blend
- BBQ spice
- Nutritional yeast
- Coffee
- Vanilla extract
- Coconut oil
- Avocado oil
- Butter
- Mayonnaise

Purchase the following:

Items:	Store:	Quantity:	Price:
Large White Eggs, 12 count, 24 oz.	Walmart	1	1.38
Almond milk, 0.5 gal	Walmart	1	1.75
Cheddar cheese 8 oz.	Walmart	1	1.6
Beef Eye Round Steak, 1.33 lb. count 4	Walmart	1	5.2
Chicken drumsticks, 5 lb. count 13	Walmart	1	4.5
Kale bunch	Walmart	1	0.6
Brussels sprouts 12 oz.	Walmart	1	1.1
Turkey bacon 12 oz.	Walmart	1	2.1
Broccoli and cauliflower 12 oz.	Walmart	1	1
Green onion bunch	Walmart	1	0.5
Lime, count 1	Walmart	1	0.25
		Total:	19.98

Day 78

Breakfast – Egg Wraps

Serving: 2
Preparation time: 5 minutes; Cooking time: 5 minutes;
Nutritional Info: 68 Cal; 4.7 g Fats; 5.5 g Protein; 0.5 g Net Carb; 0 g Fiber;
Ingredients
- 2 eggs, pasteurized
- 1 tablespoon coconut oil

Extra:
- ¼ teaspoon salt
- 1/8 teaspoon ground black pepper

Directions
3. Take a medium bowl, crack eggs in it, add salt and black pepper, and then whisk until blended.
4. Take a frying pan, place it over medium-low heat, add coconut oil and when it melts, pour in half of the egg, spread it evenly into a thin layer by rotating the pan and cook for 2 minutes.
5. Then flip the pan, cook for 1 minute, and transfer to a plate.
6. Repeat with the remaining egg to make another wrap, then roll each egg wrap and serve.

Lunch – Sprouts Stir-fry with Kale, Broccoli, and Beef

Serving: 2
Preparation time: 5 minutes; Cooking time: 8 minutes;
Nutritional Info: 125 Cal; 9.4 g Fats; 4.8 g Protein; 1.7 g Net Carb; 2.6 g Fiber;
Ingredients
- 3 slices of beef roast, chopped
- 2 ounces Brussels sprouts, halved
- 4 ounces broccoli florets
- 3 ounces kale
- 1 ½ tablespoon butter, unsalted
- 1/8 teaspoon red pepper flakes

Extra:
- ¼ teaspoon garlic powder
- ¼ teaspoon salt
- 1/8 teaspoon ground black pepper

Directions
4. Take a medium skillet pan, place it over medium heat, add ¾ tablespoons butter and when it melts, add broccoli florets and sprouts, sprinkle with garlic powder, and cook for 2 minutes.
5. Season vegetables with salt and red pepper flakes, add chopped beef, stir until mixed and continue cooking for 3 minutes until browned on one side.
6. Then add kale along with remaining butter, flip the vegetables and cook for 2 minutes until kale leaves wilts.
7. Serve straight away.

Dinner – Steak and Cheese Plate

Serving: 2
Preparation time: 5 minutes; Cooking time: 10 minutes;
Nutritional Info: 714 Cal; 65.3 g Fats; 25.3 g Protein; 4 g Net Carb; 5.3 g Fiber;
Ingredients
- 1 green onion, chopped
- 2 ounces chopped lettuce
- 2 beef steaks, grass-fed
- 2 ounces of cheddar cheese, sliced

- ½ cup mayonnaise

Extra:

- ¼ teaspoon salt
- 1/8 teaspoon ground black pepper
- 3 tablespoons avocado oil

Directions

8. Prepare the steak, and for this, season it with salt and black pepper.
9. Take a medium skillet pan, place it over medium heat, add oil and when hot, add seasoned steaks, and cook for 7 to 10 minutes until cooked to the desired level.
10. When done, distribute steaks between two plates, add scallion, lettuce, and cheese slices.
11. Drizzle with remaining oil and then serve with mayonnaise.

Day 79

Breakfast – Chaffles with Poached Eggs

Serving: 2
Preparation time: 5 minutes; Cooking time: 10 minutes;
Nutritional Info: 265 Cal; 18.5 g Fats; 17.6 g Protein; 3.4 g Net Carb; 6 g Fiber;
Ingredients

- 2 teaspoons coconut flour
- ½ cup shredded cheddar cheese, full-fat
- 3 eggs, pasteurized

Extra:

- ¼ teaspoon salt
- 1/8 teaspoon ground black pepper

Directions

1. Switch on a mini waffle maker and let it preheat for 5 minutes.
2. Meanwhile, take a medium bowl, place all the ingredients in it, reserving 2 eggs and then mix by using an immersion blender until smooth.
3. Ladle the batter evenly into the waffle maker, shut with lid, and let it cook for 3 to 4 minutes until firm and golden brown.
4. Meanwhile, prepare poached eggs, and for this, take a medium bowl half full with water, place it over medium heat and bring it to a boil.
5. Then crack an egg in a ramekin, carefully pour it into the boiling water and cook for 3 minutes.
6. Transfer egg to a plate lined with paper towels by using a slotted spoon and repeat with the other egg.
7. Top chaffles with poached eggs, season with salt and black pepper, and then serve.

Lunch – Oven Fried Cheddar Cauliflower and Broccoli Florets

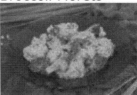

Serving: 2
Preparation time: 5 minutes; Cooking time: 15 minutes;
Nutritional Info: 185 Cal; 14.1 g Fats; 7.7 g Protein; 3.9 g Net Carb; 2 g Fiber;
Ingredients

- 6 ounces cauliflower and broccoli florets

- ½ teaspoon garlic powder
- 1 tablespoon coconut oil, melted
- 2 tablespoons grated cheddar cheese
- ½ egg, pasteurized, beaten

Extra:
- ¼ teaspoon salt

Directions
1. Switch on the oven, then set it to 400 degrees F and let it preheat.
2. Take a small bowl, crack the egg in it, add garlic powder, salt, and coconut oil and whisk until blended.
3. Take a medium bowl, place add florets in it, pour egg batter on florets, toss until well coated, and then mix in cheese.
4. Take a baking sheet, grease it with oil, spread florets mixture on it in a single layer, and then bake for 10 to 15 minutes until vegetables have turned tender and nicely browned.
5. Serve straight away.

Dinner – Spiced Chicken Drumsticks

Serving: 2
Preparation time: 5 minutes; Cooking time: 15 minutes;
Nutritional Info: 275 Cal; 14.1 g Fats; 35.2 g Protein; 0.6 g Net Carb; 0.1 g Fiber;
Ingredients
- 2 chicken drumsticks, drumsticks
- ½ teaspoon garlic powder
- ½ teaspoon onion powder
- ½ teaspoon smoked paprika
- 1 tablespoon avocado oil

Extra:
- ¼ teaspoon salt
- ¼ teaspoon ground black pepper

Directions
5. Switch on the oven, then set it to 400 degrees F and let it preheat.
6. Meanwhile, take a plastic bag, place all the ingredients in it, seal the bag and turn it upside down to coat chicken with the spices.
7. Take a pan, place chicken on it, and then bake for 10 to 15 minutes until cooked through and browned, turning halfway.
8. Serve straight away.

Day 80

Breakfast – Scrambled Eggs with Kale

Serving: 2
Preparation time: 5 minutes; Cooking time: 8 minutes;
Nutritional Info: 173 Cal; 14.5 g Fats; 8.5 g Protein; 1.2 g Net Carb; 0.1 g Fiber;
Ingredients
- 1 green onion, chopped
- ½ cup chopped kale
- 1 tablespoon avocado oil
- 2 eggs
- 1 tablespoon grated cheddar cheese

Extra:
- 1/8 teaspoon garlic powder
- ¼ teaspoon salt

Directions
5. Take a medium skillet pan, place it over medium heat, add oil and when hot, add green onion and cook for 1 minute until tender-crisp.
6. Add kale, season with garlic powder and salt, stir until mixed and cook for 1 minute until kale leaves wilt.
7. Crack eggs in a bowl, whisk until well combined, then pour the egg into the pan, spread evenly, and cook for 2 minutes until it begins to set, don't stir.
8. Then scramble the eggs and continue cooking for 2 to 3 minutes until eggs have cooked to the desired level.
9. Sprinkle with cheese and then serve.

Lunch – Garlic Brussels sprouts with Bacon

Serving: 2
Preparation time: 5 minutes; Cooking time: 15 minutes;
Nutritional Info: 202 Cal; 15.1 g Fats; 7.7 g Protein; 3.9 g Net Carb; 2.4 g Fiber;
Ingredients
- 3 slices of bacon, pasteurized
- 4 ounces Brussels sprouts, halved
- 2 green onions, diced
- ¾ tablespoon butter, unsalted
- 2 tablespoons chicken broth

Extra:
- ½ teaspoon garlic powder
- ¼ teaspoon salt
- ¾ tablespoon avocado oil

Directions
4. Take a medium skillet pan, place it over medium heat, add oil and wait until it gets hot.
5. Cut bacon slices into squares, add to the skillet pan and cook for 2 to 3 minutes until bacon fat starts to render.
6. Transfer bacon pieces to a plate lined with paper towels and then set aside until required.
7. Add butter into the skillet pan and when it starts to brown, add onion, sprinkle with garlic powder and cook for 1 minute or more until semi-translucent.
8. Add sprouts, season with salt, stir until mixed and cook for 2 to 3 minutes until beginning to brown.
9. Pour in chicken broth, stir until mixed and cook for 5 to 7 minutes until broth is absorbed, covering the pan.
10. Then make a hole in the center of pan by pushing sprouts to the side of the pan, add bacon and stir until well mixed.
11. Serve straight away.

Dinner – Garlicky Steaks with Rosemary

Serving: 2
Preparation time: 25 minutes; Cooking time: 12 minutes;
Nutritional Info: 213 Cal; 13 g Fats; 22 g Protein; 1 g Net Carb; 0 g Fiber;
Ingredients
- 2 beef steaks
- 1/4 of a lime, juiced

- 1 ½ teaspoon garlic powder
- ¾ teaspoon dried rosemary
- 2 ½ tablespoons avocado oil

Extra:

- ½ teaspoon salt
- ¼ teaspoon ground black pepper

Directions

4. Prepare steaks, and for this, sprinkle garlic powder on all sides of steak.

5. Take a shallow dish, place 1 ½ tablespoon oil and lime juice in it, whisk until combined, add steaks, turn to coat and let it marinate for 20 minutes at room temperature.

6. Then take a griddle pan, place it over medium-high heat and grease it with remaining oil.

7. Season marinated steaks with salt and black pepper, add to the griddle pan and cook for 7 to 12 minutes until cooked to the desired level.

8. When done, wrap steaks in foil for 5 minutes, then cut into slices across the grain.

9. Sprinkle rosemary over steaks slices and then serve.

Day 81

Breakfast – Coconut Flax Porridge

Serving: 2
Preparation time: 5 minutes; Cooking time: 5 minutes;
Nutritional Info: 403 Cal; 32.2 g Fats; 12.1 g Protein; 3 g Net Carb; 13.2 g Fiber;
Ingredients

- 3 ounces coconut flour
- 1 tablespoon ground flaxseed
- 1/8 teaspoon salt
- 2 cups water, boiling
- 2 tablespoons whipped cream

Extra:

- 3 tablespoons chopped almonds
- 6 tablespoons almond milk, unsweetened

Directions

3. Take a large heatproof bowl, place coconut flour in it and then stir in flaxseed and salt until mixed.

4. Pour in boiling water, stir until combined, and then microwave for 1 minute at high heat setting until thickened.

5. Distribute porridge between two bowls, stir in almond milk, top with almonds and cream, and then serve.

Lunch – Cheesy Spicy Broccoli and Cauliflower Rice

Serving: 2
Preparation time: 5 minutes; Cooking time: 12 minutes;
Nutritional Info: 288 Cal; 25.3 g Fats; 5.8 g Protein; 5.5 g Net Carb; 3.9 g Fiber;
Ingredients

- 3 ounces cauliflower florets, grated
- 3 ounces broccoli florets, chopped
- ½ tablespoon BBQ spice
- 1 ½ tablespoon avocado oil
- 2 tablespoons grated cheddar cheese

Directions

5. Take a medium pot, place it over medium-low heat, add ¾ tablespoon oil and when hot, stir in the cauliflower and cook for 5 to 7 minutes until tender and golden brown.

6. Meanwhile, take a medium heatproof bowl, place broccoli florets in it, cover with a plastic wrap, and then microwave for 2 minutes until steams.

7. Drain the steamed broccoli florets, add it to the pot, add

oil and cheese, sprinkle with BBQ spice, stir well and cook for 2 minutes until cheese has melted.

8. Serve straight away.

Dinner – Chili Lime Baked Chicken Legs

Serving: 2
Preparation time: 5 minutes; Cooking time: 10 minutes;
Nutritional Info: 248 Cal; 19 g Fats; 14 g Protein; 0 g Net Carb; 0 g Fiber;
Ingredients

- 2 chicken drumsticks, pasteurized
- ½ teaspoon red chili powder
- ½ teaspoon smoked paprika
- ¼ of a lime, juiced
- 1 ½ tablespoon avocado oil

Extra:

- 1/3 teaspoon salt
- ¼ teaspoon ground black pepper

Directions

6. Switch on the oven, then set it to 450 degrees F and let it preheat.
7. Prepare the marinade and for this, take a small bowl, place salt, black pepper, red chili powder, paprika, lime juice, and oil in it and then stir until well combined.
8. Brush the marinade generously on all sides of chicken and then let marinate for 20 minutes.
9. When the chicken has marinated, take a baking sheet, line it with aluminum foil, place a cookie rack on it, then place marinated chicken on it and bake for 15 to 20 minutes until thoroughly cooked and crisp, turning halfway.
10. Serve straight away.

Day 82
Breakfast – Latte

Serving: 2
Preparation time: 5 minutes; Cooking time: 0 minutes;
Nutritional Info: 191 Cal; 18 g Fats; 6 g Protein; 1 g Net Carb; 0 g Fiber;
Ingredients

- 1 teaspoon pumpkin pie spice
- ¼ teaspoon vanilla extract, unsweetened
- 2 eggs
- 2 tablespoons coconut oil

- 1 ½ cup water, boiling

Directions

8. Place all the ingredients in the order into a food processor or a blender and then pulse for 2 to 3 minutes until smooth.
9. Serve immediately.

Lunch – Sprouts Gratin with Bacon

Serving: 2
Preparation time: 10 minutes; Cooking time: 30 minutes;
Nutritional Info: 196 Cal; 15 g Fats; 8 g Protein; 5 g Net Carb; 3 g Fiber;
Ingredients

- 4 ounces Brussels sprouts, halved
- 2 slices of bacon, chopped, cooked
- 2 tablespoons almond milk, unsweetened
- 2 tablespoons coconut cream
- 3 tablespoons grated cheddar cheese

Extra:

- 1/3 teaspoon salt

- 1/3 teaspoon ground black pepper
- ½ tablespoon butter, unsalted
- 1 tablespoon avocado oil

Directions

4. Switch on the oven, then set it to 400 degrees F and let it preheat.
5. Take a baking pan, line it with aluminum foil, place Brussels sprouts in it, drizzle with oil, and season with 1/4 teaspoon each of salt and black pepper.
6. Spread sprouts in a single layer and then roast for 15 t0 20 minutes until crispy and edges turned browned, stirring halfway.
7. Meanwhile, prepare the sauce, and for this, take a medium heatproof bowl, place butter in it, and then microwave for 1 minute or more until it melts.
8. Add milk and cream, whisk until combined, and microwave for 1 minute until hot.
9. Add 2 tablespoons of cheese along with remaining salt and black pepper and stir until mixed.

10. When sprouts have roasted, transfer them into a small pan, pour prepared sauce over sprouts, sprinkle with bacon and remaining cheese, and then bake for 5 to 10 minutes until bubbly and top have turned golden brown.
11. Serve straight away.

Dinner – Garlicky Salt and Pepper Chicken

Serving: 2
Preparation time: 5 minutes; Cooking time: 12 minutes;
Nutritional Info: 320 Cal; 18.5 g Fats; 34 g Protein; 1.9 g Net Carb; 0.5 g Fiber;
Ingredients

- 2 chicken drumsticks
- 2 green onions, diced
- 1 ½ tsp garlic powder
- ½ tsp red pepper flakes
- 2 tsps sesame oil

Extra:

- ½ tsp salt
- 1/3 tsp ground black pepper
- 1 tablespoon avocado oil

Directions

7. Switch on the oven, then set it to 400 degrees F and let it preheat.
8. Meanwhile, take a small bowl, place salt and black pepper in it, and then stir until mixed.
9. Take a small baking sheet, grease it with avocado oil, place chicken drumsticks on it, season with the salt-pepper mixture until coated completely and then bake for 10 to 12 minutes until cooked and crispy, turning halfway.
10. When chicken is almost cooked, take a small skillet pan, place it over medium-low heat, add sesame oil and when hot, add onion, sprinkle with garlic powder and cook for 3 to 4 minutes until golden brown.
11. When the chicken has baked, transfer it to a medium bowl, drizzle with garlic-onion oil and toss until coated.
12. Transfer chicken to a dish, top with garlic-onion mixture, and then serve.

Day 83

Breakfast – Spicy Flaxseed Wraps

Serving: 2
Preparation time: 5 minutes; Cooking time: 10 minutes;
Nutritional Info: 270 Cal; 24.3 g Fats; 4.7 g Protein; 0.4 g Net Carb; 7.7 g Fiber;
Ingredients
- 1/3 cup ground flaxseeds
- 1/8 teaspoon ginger powder
- 1/8 teaspoon garlic powder
- ½ cup of water
- 2 tablespoons avocado oil

Extra:
- ¼ teaspoon salt

Directions
4. Take a small saucepan, place it over medium heat, pour in water, and bring it to a boil.
5. Remove pan from heat, add garlic, ginger, salt, and flaxseeds and stir until well combined and the dough comes together.
6. Transfer dough to a clean working space lined with parchment paper, divide it into two portions and shape each portion into a ball.
7. Working on each dough ball at a time, cover with another piece of parchment paper and then roll 0.1-inch thick round wrap and when done, remove the parchment paper on top.
8. Take a medium skillet pan, place it over medium-high heat, add 1 tablespoon oil and when hot, place a prepared wrap and cook for 2 minutes per side until golden.
9. Repeat with the other wrap and serve it straight away or with favorite filling.

Lunch – Buttery Bacon Brussel Sprouts

Serving: 2
Preparation time: 5 minutes; Cooking time: 10 minutes;
Nutritional Info: 278 Cal; 24.7 g Fats; 7.6 g Protein; 3.9 g Net Carb; 2.4 g Fiber;
Ingredients
- 4 ounces Brussels sprouts, halved
- 3 slices of turkey bacon, chopped
- 1 teaspoon garlic powder
- ¼ of a lime, zested
- 3 tablespoons butter, unsalted

Extra:
- 1 tablespoon chopped walnut

Directions
7. Take a small saucepan half full with water, place it over medium heat, and bring it to a boil.
8. Add sprouts, cook for 5 minutes until just cooked and then drain into a colander.
9. Take a frying pan, place it over medium heat, add butter and when it melts, add bacon and cook for 3 to 4 minutes until crispy.
10. Sprinkle with ½ teaspoon garlic, cook for 30 seconds until fragrant, and then sprinkle with lime zest.
11. Add sprouts, stir until mixed, toss until well coated, and cook for 1 minute until hot.
12. Garnish with walnuts and serve.

Dinner – Smoked Paprika Drumsticks

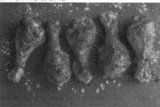

Serving: 2
Preparation time: 5 minutes; Cooking time: 20 minutes;
Nutritional Info: 200 Cal; 12 g Fats; 20 g Protein; 2 g Net Carb; 1 g Fiber;
Ingredients
- 2 chicken drumsticks, pasteurized
- ¼ tablespoon smoked paprika
- ¼ teaspoon onion powder
- 2 tablespoons butter, unsalted, melted
- 2/3 tablespoon nutritional yeast

Extra:
- ¼ teaspoon salt
- 1/8 teaspoon ground black pepper
- 1/8 teaspoon cayenne pepper
- ¼ teaspoon garlic powder

Directions
6. Switch on the oven, then set it to 350 degrees F and let it preheat.
7. Take a plastic bag, add chicken in it, add remaining ingredients except for butter, seal the bag, and shake it well to coat chicken with the spice.
8. Take a baking sheet, line it with foil, place a cookie sheet on it, then place chicken on it and cook for 10 minutes.
9. Then brush chicken with melted butter and continue baking for 5 to 10 minutes until crispy.
10. Serve straight away.

Day 84

Breakfast – Bulletproof Coffee with Cream

Serving: 2
Preparation time: 5 minutes; Cooking time: 0 minutes;
Nutritional Info: 421 Cal; 47 g Fats; 1.9 g Protein; 6.9 g Net Carb; 1.7 g Fiber;
Ingredients
- 2 cups brewed coffee
- 2 tbsps coconut cream
- 2 tbsps coconut oil
- 2 tablespoon butter, unsalted

Directions
3. Place all the ingredients in the order into a food processor or blender and then pulse for 1 to 2 minutes until foamy.
4. Divide coffee among two mugs and then serve.

Lunch – Broccoli and Cauliflower Nuggets

Serving: 2
Preparation time: 10 minutes; Cooking time: 10 minutes;
Nutritional Info: 483.5 Cal; 46.7 g Fats; 9.7 g Protein; 2.2 g Net Carb; 3.9 g Fiber;
Ingredients
- 2 tbsps almond flour
- 4 ounces broccoli and cauliflower florets
- 2 tbsps grated cheddar cheese
- 2 tbsps ground flaxseed meal
- ½ of an egg

Extra:
- 1/3 teaspoon salt
- ¼ teaspoon ground black pepper
- 2 tbsps avocado oil
- ¼ cup mayonnaise

Directions
5. Place cauliflower and broccoli florets into a medium heatproof bowl, cover with a plastic wrap, and then microwave for 2 to 3 minutes at high heat setting until steamed.
6. Drain the florets, transfer them to a food processor, add cheese, flaxseed, salt, black pepper, and egg, and then pulse for 1 to 2 minutes until smooth.
7. Tip the mixture into a bowl, shape it into small balls, flatten them into the shape of nugget and then coat with almond flour.
8. Take a frying pan, place it over medium heat, add oil and when hot, place prepared nuggets on it, and then cook for 3 minutes per side until golden brown.
9. Serve nuggets with mayonnaise.

Dinner – Herb Roasted
Chicken Drumsticks

Serving: 2
Preparation time: 5
minutes; Cooking time: 12
minutes;
Nutritional Info: 377 Cal;
27 g Fats; 27 g Protein; 4
g Net Carb; 1 g Fiber;
Ingredients
- 2 chicken
  drumsticks
- ¼ of a lime, juiced
- ½ teaspoon Italian
  herb blend
- ½ teaspoon garlic
  powder
- 2 tbsps avocado oil
Extra:
- 1/3 teaspoon salt
Directions
5. Switch on the
   oven, then set it to
   400 degrees F and
   let it preheat.
6. Meanwhile, place
   chicken into a
   bowl, add
   remaining
   ingredients except
   for oil and toss
   until well coated.
7. Transfer chicken
   drumsticks into a
   baking sheet
   greased with
   avocado oil and
   then bake for 10 to
   12 minutes until
   cooked and slightly
   crispy, turning
   halfway.
8. Serve straight
   away.

Made in the USA
Monee, IL
04 February 2020